TRANSFORMING FIRE

THEOLOGICAL EDUCATION BETWEEN THE TIMES

Ted A. Smith, series editor

Theological Education between the Times gathers diverse groups of people for critical, theological conversations about the meanings and purposes of theological education in a time of deep change. The project is funded by the Lilly Endowment Inc.

TRANSFORMING FIRE

Imagining Christian Teaching

Mark D. Jordan

WILLIAM B. EERDMANS PUBLISHING COMPANY

GRAND RAPIDS, MICHIGAN

Wm. B. Eerdmans Publishing Co.
4035 Park East Court SE, Grand Rapids, Michigan 49546
www.eerdmans.com

Published 2021
Printed in the United States of America

27 26 25 24 23 22 21   1 2 3 4 5 6 7

ISBN 978-0-8028-7903-5

Library of Congress Cataloging-in-Publication Data

Names: Jordan, Mark D., author.
Title: Transforming fire : imagining Christian teaching / Mark D.
    Jordan.
Description: Grand Rapids, Michigan : William B. Eerdmans Publish-
    ing Company, 2021. | Series: Theological education between the
    times | Includes bibliographical references. | Summary: "Med-
    itations on pedagogy in Christian education through various depic-
    tions and examples of Christian teaching in literature"—Provided
    by publisher.
Identifiers: LCCN 2020027758 | ISBN 9780802879035 (paperback)
Subjects: LCSH: Christian education.
Classification: LCC BV1471.3 .J67 2921 | DDC 268—dc23
LC record available at https://lccn.loc.gov/2020027758

Contents

CONTENTS

A Little Advice

Though I am overly fond of ironies, I still find myself wanting books to begin with a few frank words to readers, and all the more so in Christian books, with their legacies of hypocrisy and other crooked speech.

Dear Reader, this is a book on Christian teaching by someone who has suffered from too many books and not enough of them. As a young teacher, looking frantically for help, I found many books *about* teaching beside the point. Either they offered small, tidy solutions to incidental problems or they deduced a satisfied system from assumptions about what ideal Christian teaching must be.

This book offers neither solutions nor systems. It trusts instead that we still learn from the books we assign to our classes. To say that again: we don't need books *about* teaching so much as books *that teach*. So this small book tries to show how some of the available patterns of Christian teaching might still work wonders, even as institutions for theological education shrink or vanish.

I continue to be surprised by how often teaching is passed over in our fretful conversations about the future—or left to last place, as if fixing institutional arrangements would take care of it. As if you could ever finish your practice teaching.

A large part of teaching is sequence. Writing this book, I can propose a sequence but not impose it. You will read it as you choose, picking it up and setting it aside on your own schedule.

You may skip around in it—or throw it across the room in irritation. Still, here is my advice about sequence.

The first two chapters prepare for what comes after. They don't preview it or summarize it: they commend habits to get you ready for it. Consider reading them first.

The middle section of the book reactivates or restages selected scenes of Christian teaching. I arrange the scenes two by two for the sake of contrast. I label the contrasting pairs with themes: bodies, sciences, moving pictures, children, and barriers. I then insert annotations on each pair of scenes to draw out persisting tensions in Christian teaching. (Some tensions issue from paradoxes in Jesus's good news. Others register reactions of human power to divine teaching.) The printed order of the middle chapters makes sense to me, but you might want to rearrange them.

You should also remember that my selection is one of many. We have abundant records of Christian teaching. I could have written this book using an entirely different selection of texts, grouped under three headings or seven. If you don't like my choices, I urge you to assemble an anthology of your own.

The book's last section looks up from the reactivated scenes of Christian teaching toward different futures and deeper pasts. Consider reading this section last. I don't see how it makes sense to skip ahead to it. Of course, I may be wrong. Human teaching is mostly guesswork. It is like trying to anticipate a shifting wind, blowing when and where it pleases. Sometimes we catch its sound around us, but we can never tell exactly how it goes.

I apply that image also to the word "Christian," which I have already used almost a dozen times. There can be no satisfactory definition for it, whether as a claimed name or as an imposed label (compare Acts 26:28). Proposing any definition, I would encourage superficial views. (It might be worth remembering that the canonical Gospels never use it.) Let me suggest instead that we let the tired word float free, as convenient but misleading slang.

Christian Traditions and Shapes of Teaching

Forty-five years ago, I was told a story by my undergraduate mentor, who also served for a time as the college dean. He recounted it when I approached him in both of his roles to complain about classes.

A man receives jade cufflinks as an unexpected gift. Charmed, he decides to learn about the stone. Since he knows nothing, he wants to learn a lot quickly. He hears that a gem collector is offering private lessons. He meets her in an apartment overfilled with art he takes to be Chinese. They agree on payment (made in advance) and set a schedule. Some days later, the man returns for his first lesson. He's met at the door by a younger woman—an assistant?—who shows him to the living room. On the coffee table, there is a single piece of jade held gently in black velvet. She leaves him alone. Baffled, then irritated, he fidgets in front of the stone for the length of the lesson. "It's a test," he decides. "I'll prove how serious I am by sitting here this once. Then we can start the real lessons next time." One week later, the same ritual is repeated. The only difference is the stone on display. Resolved not to give up, the man decides to beat the frustrating woman at her own game, no matter how long it takes. After several more weeks, he can barely contain his irritation. He decides to bring a friend to the next lesson so that at least one other person can share his righteous anger. As always, the assistant (and who exactly is she?) leads them into the living room, where a new stone waits. *"You see what I mean!"* the man bursts out. *"This is what my so-called teacher does week after week. And, look, it's not even good jade."*

Retelling this story after four decades, I'm not sure that it still works. Can we imagine anyone tolerating so much consumer frustration before demanding a full refund and posting thumbs-down reviews online for jade shoppers? Of course, impatience is one of the story's devices. Its telling demands a little of the patience that it means to commend. How we talk about teaching is a teaching.

There are other points in the story. One is, learning begins best in desire. That desire will change as you progress, but it has to remain strong enough to withstand frustration. A teacher may well shift from an object of respect to a cause of exasperation, because provoking resentment is one thing teachers must do for students.[1] The story's biggest lesson remains the punch line: students often learn the most important things without recognizing that they have been taught.

If you find the story about the jade contrived, you might prefer a historical anecdote. The zoologist Louis Agassiz once asked a new student to spend time with fish after the student declared a specialty in insects. Handing over a fish, he left the student mostly alone, returning from time to time to ask what had been noticed. When the student inquired, timidly, what came next, Agassiz replied, "Look at your fish." After some days, another fish of a related variety was added for comparison. Eight months later, the student was told to move on to insects—though he now found himself reluctant to leave the fish.[2]

Agassiz's way of teaching may seem intolerably authoritarian. He disregards the student's expressed interests, imposes other lessons without justification, and is frustratingly coy in both his presences and his absences. You can imagine the reactions in our present setting. The student evaluations will be awful, and it is highly unlikely that any temporary teaching-contract will be renewed. (Note to "senior" faculty: the need to curry instant favor with students inhibits teaching. Teachers in the most precarious positions are not only impoverished, they are prevented from teaching forcefully.)

Still, what strikes me is how much scope Agassiz gives to the student. There is the freedom to get up and walk out, of course. There is also freedom for curiosity, improvisation, abrupt change of direction, or ungraded failure. No syllabus calendar meters progress. No course objectives must be checked off. There is not even a fixed body of facts to be acquired. Agassiz is trying to teach the student to see—that is, to learn how to learn. To stay in the room, to sit with the fish, the student must trust Agassiz as a teacher. The trust is not in Agassiz's pronouncements but in his pedagogy. The authority of the teaching is not secured by certified expertise, voluminous publications, or status in the guild. It is vindicated in the student's transformation. The student grants Agassiz pedagogical authority by changing. Or Agassiz grows in authority by responding to the student's inarticulate, half-known intellectual passion.

> **Exercise**: Imagine retelling the Agassiz story about someone who wants to learn not jade or insects but God. Which specimens should an astute teacher place before that kind of student?
>
> **Exercise**: Imagine that a student comes to the gem collector to learn not so much about jade as about varnished paintings of jade jewelry. Or imagine the conversation between Louis Agassiz and a student who arrives intent on mastering the colored plates in Cuvier's *Natural History of Fish* (published 1828–1849). Would Agassiz direct the student to the library's rare book room, or would he suggest, slyly, that the engravings might make more sense after the student had devoted a little time to looking at real fish?
>
> **Questions for reflection**: Is teaching Christian theology in our between-time more like teaching about jade or about old paintings of jade? Do most students of theology want the

slimy uncertainties of fish or numbered plates of collect-
ible engravings? And what do we teachers want—for the
students, for ourselves? How many of us hope to meet a
living God?

Teaching "Christian Tradition"

Over the course of four decades or so, I have earned a living by
teaching what catalogues call "the Christian tradition." The
phrase is likely to mislead. Inherited Christian teachings are
never singular, never one "tradition." They throw off variations.
Variations become disagreements. Persistent disagreements
lead to bitter controversies about what counts as Christian or
who gets to use that name. It would be more exact to say that
I have taught "influential books that claim to hand on some
Christian truth." Even that rephrasing begs the question whether
students are more interested in the books or in the truth they
might offer.

Another trouble with my self-description is the assumption
that any Christian tradition *can* be taught—indeed, taught pro-
fessionally, predictably, as a career. I have been hired to teach
Christian tradition because schools of various kinds require it for
the degrees they offer. They squeeze the desire to learn through
degree requirements—not to speak of rules for ordination. For
many students, no doubt, my classes have been episodes in earn-
ing credentials. (What do you desire to *learn* when you desire a degree?) The licensing requirements fix the content on offer. Before
reaching college, I read catalogues greedily in naïve confidence
that a one-semester course would actually give me "a complete
survey of Christian thought" or "major figures of contemporary
theology." I didn't yet understand that course descriptions are
habitual fictions—when they are not vain boasts.

I also couldn't appreciate how differently competing institutions decide the content of "Christian tradition." My paid
teaching began at a large state university famous for football.
The job was "teaching assistant" in a philosophy course about

(Christian) ideas of God. Some Christian books were slipped into a state-sponsored curriculum as canonical readings for Western philosophy. I then moved to an integrated humanities program in a Catholic university—also known for football. For that program, books of the "Christian tradition" were both masterpieces of the liberal arts and expressions of Catholic Identity (very much capitalized). Next came the philosophy department of a smaller Catholic university—a college, really—where I was expected to teach undergraduates and seminarians a perennial philosophy according to Thomas Aquinas. On a barren hilltop, surrounded by stubby post oak and mesquite, Catholic Intellectual Identity meant faithfulness to Saint Thomas for philosophy and to Flannery O'Connor for most everything else. In later years, I taught at a pontifical faculty that had once concentrated on medieval Christian thought as a remedy for modern fragmentation. Later still, I was hired into a large research university founded by Methodists and so still committed to the study of religion, including the training of professional ministers. In these latter days, I have moved to the faculty of an all-too-famous research university dedicated to forming citizen-leaders. Here the teaching of Christian tradition is permitted because it might still prove helpful for managing the world.

The reader should hear humor in this very partial recounting of my career. Humor and some sobering self-knowledge. Let me add, a bit more seriously, two reminders. At every institution that has employed me, there have been remarkable students, generous colleagues, and more good books in the library than I could read (no matter how beggared the budget for acquisitions). Clutching at academic grandeur, we can fail to notice the prospects for teaching right around us. Here is the other reminder: along this unplanned itinerary, my education in teaching continued without interruption. Whatever the curriculum or degree requirements, however rancorous the faculty politics, each classroom offered lessons to all who entered it.

As I negotiated competing specifications of "Christian tradition," I began to notice unexpected commonalities. Wherever

I teach older Christian texts, I push against shared assumptions about teaching that lie underneath most US curricula modeled on "the humanities." (We should still do a double take whenever theology is subsumed by the humanities.) For standard courses, there is a minimum required number of hours of "classroom contact." Student progress is measured at fixed intervals in quantifiable ways. Classroom decorum limits rather strictly the things students can be encouraged to say, to feel, or to do. They are enrolled to acquire information, to practice skills, to clarify their own values—but not to be spiritually transformed. Of the accusations made against religion in secularized universities, none is more damning than the charge that it proselytizes. (Imagine a similar suspicion applied to ardent advocates of Shakespeare or Foucault.) A university course in religion is too often a narrow mail slot through which content of approved sizes is delivered on a regular schedule. In some cases, it also serves as a decontamination chamber for scrubbing religions of whatever makes them religious.

Of course, none of my employing institutions could control what actually happened in their classrooms when certain authors were let loose. A strong text violates the rules or expectations. Beginning with the Bible, inherited Christian books are designed to open spaces for learning beyond professional training or standardized "liberal education." Please note that I'm not pointing to the supposed differences between "descriptive" and "normative" or "tolerant" and "dogmatic." (Those binaries are neither coherent nor helpful.) The immediate tensions between the containing classroom and the Christian books within it have more to do with things like the allotment of time, the role of emotion, changes in bodily movements, and practices of attention. The most influential Christian texts set forth the means by which their lessons are to be taught. They give their own accounts of how they can best be handed down (which is, after all, the root meaning of the Latin word *traditio*).

You can show up to learn about engravings, but certain authors will keep plopping fish down on your desk.

Christian Traditions in University Classrooms

I am hardly the first person to notice tensions between Christian traditions and university classrooms. Two hundred years ago, they were familiar enough to teachers who wanted to save a place for the advanced study of Christianity within new European universities.

The most familiar example is probably the founding of the (Humboldt) University of Berlin in 1811. Friedrich Schleiermacher is a key figure, though neither the first nor perhaps the most effective. He is credited with formulating a durable argument for keeping Christian theology within modern universities. Though I disagree with his argument, I will follow his vocabulary. Here and in the rest of the book, I use "theology" roughly as Schleiermacher does: it names the whole of what might be taught as Christian tradition, including the varied fields offered by a "divinity school" or "seminary." I acknowledge the sharp disagreements about what those fields actually are. My account of teaching should be wide enough to cover many of the alternatives.

Back to Schleiermacher in Berlin. Six hundred years earlier, theology had entered some of the original European universities as one of the constitutive faculties. It stood alongside medicine and law as an advanced course of study after the liberal arts. The price of admission for getting theology into medieval universities? Adopting a guild model for teaching it. The compromise was not entirely successful. (Theology's place among the faculties was never as settled as it can seem to the critic or defender of institutional forms.) For Schleiermacher, the pressing question was whether the medieval arrangement should survive the growth of natural science, antichurch philosophies, and the sharp-eyed interests of the modern nation-state.

Schleiermacher first published his views on the topic telegraphically, as propositions or theses. They are easy to misunderstand, especially for readers who haven't learned his idiosyncratic vocabulary. They are also strategic proposals in a negotiation. Still, even a hasty reading makes a few things clear. The theology that Schleiermacher wants to keep in universities is defined as a body of knowledge, the science (*Wissenschaft*) required for church leadership. As an expert in such knowledge, a university professor of theology is obliged to contribute to corresponding fields elsewhere in the university. As a member of the faculty of theology, a professor must share in the distinctive purpose of training future church leaders.[3] The various topics in theology are held together only as a response to a practical and political problem—namely, staffing churches. (Though he wishes it were otherwise, Schleiermacher assumes that clergy appointments will involve the state.) Without that purpose, the various pieces of theological knowledge would scatter back to their corresponding fields in the other faculties.

Even when it is read hastily, Schleiermacher's early text explains why discussions of "theological education" often focus only on clergy training, as if the two topics were interchangeable. He cannot be blamed for inventing that confusion. In churches with exclusive theologies of priesthood, theology's secrets were frequently restricted to the ordained. Schleiermacher shows how it is possible to arrive at a similar restriction from professional principles. Whenever it begins, and however it is justified, the reduction of theology to ministerial formation is unfortunate. Among other consequences, it cuts out much of the inheritance of Christian writing. Many influential books now used to train clergy were written for wider audiences. Their authors found the unity of theology in more embracing aims—say, in the hope of leading all human souls toward God. Theology can be the intellectual vocation of any adult Christian.

Schleiermacher balances the professional unity of the theology faculty with its place in the whole university. Each component of university theology must maintain its connections to corresponding fields in other faculties: biblical interpretation connects to classics or Near Eastern languages, Christian ethics to philosophical ethics, and so on. The relation is so close that each theological field is pulled back into its corresponding field elsewhere if theology loses its unifying purpose of professional education. (The history of some university-based divinity schools in the United States confirms the point.) "Without this [unifying] relation this same information ceases to be theological and each aspect of it devolves to some other science" (introduction #6, p. 250). Schleiermacher secures intellectual respectability for the parts of university theology by subordinating them to other faculties. The subordination has consequences. For example, topics in university theology must be cut up according to the patterns of their counterpart sciences in the university at large. The content of each topic will also change with shifts in the corresponding field. Church history will soon become whatever academic history now is. It must abandon distinctively Christian ideas about historical processes or styles of history writing. If church historians resist the prevailing standards in the university's department of history, they risk cutting off the faculty of theology from the rest of the university—and so undermining the pact that tolerates theology anywhere within the modern university.

The scope of this pact is displayed in the opening words of Schleiermacher's first version of his basic argument: "Theology is a positive *Wissenschaft* . . ." It would take some effort to recover his exact sense of "positive." I emphasize instead the word *Wissenschaft*, "science" or body of knowledge. Theology must become *Wissenschaft* to get through the university gates. Its transformation or redefinition excludes many traditional notions about Christian teaching. For example, to call theology *Wissenschaft* means that it is not conveyed primarily through symbols or rituals.[4] It is not taught chiefly in "literary" genres or by bodily habituation—the way one might begin to teach sitting meditation or Japanese tea. So far as *Wissenschaft* remains the watchword of the modern university, theological instruction in faculties of divinity cannot be taught principally by liturgy, allegorical interpretation, or bodily practice. It cannot be handed down by visionary transmission or the repeated meditation of texts that shatter language. Yet teachers of Christian theology have depended on each of these means.

I add, on Schleiermacher's behalf, that he never imagined that the modern university would be the only place for pursuing theology. His own example points in other directions. He wrote in a range of rhetorical registers, especially in the splendid and fully "literary" *Speeches on Religion to Its Cultured Despisers*. In his dialogue *Christmas Eve*, the story of an intimate household celebration discloses a poignant theology of incarnation. Schleiermacher's academic proposal does not describe all theological teaching or writing. It is a strategy for dealing with new universities constructed around particular models of knowledge. Unfortunately, versions of the proposal have become the norm in theological education more generally. Its expectations have crept into other Christian institutions—through university training of seminary teachers, accrediting agencies, changing expectations around credentials, and so on. What is more striking, many advocates of university-based theology still rehearse versions of Schleiermacher's arguments and tailor curricula to something like his assumptions. The exclusions required to secure theology a place in the modern university have become general norms for any theology that wants to be educationally respectable.

I realize, of course, that "the modern university" is not a single thing frozen just at the moment Schleiermacher first wrote about these questions. Modern American universities now include a much wider range of teaching styles than figured in plans for the university in Berlin. Other debates since Schleiermacher have expanded the fields a university is expected to accommodate. In the 1950s, for example, there was national discussion about the introduction of studio art courses and the faculty positions needed to staff them. Similar controversies have surrounded the rise since 1950 of university-based creative-writing programs—or career training and marketable skills. I wonder whether the old anxiety of intellectual respectability prevents news of these innovations from reaching some precincts where theology is taught according to alien models of "rigor."

Still, I rehearse the story about Schleiermacher and the new university to draw other conclusions. I believe that the future of Christian theological education is roughly the reverse of what he proposed. He offered, if only as a strategy, the model of a university faculty of theology held together by the professional goals of ministerial formation. The disciplinary content of its curriculum and its forms of teaching were to be borrowed from the rest of the university. If that were the only reason for having a university faculty of theology (or seminaries modeled after it), the collapse of professional models of ministry would render them pointless. But the surviving faculties do have a point within universities and the larger economies of knowledge. In my experience, seminaries and divinity schools can also be like underground cisterns of displaced but still alluring forms of teaching. They can serve as sites of resistance to the trivialization of teaching implied by so many professional models. University faculties of theology and the seminaries linked to them sometimes conspire in forms of teaching that are strong alternatives to reductive emphases on information transfer. Theological education can be—should be—distinguished by resistant pedagogies. Or so I urge.

> **Exercise:** Rewrite Schleiermacher around a different analogy for enfranchising theology within contemporary universities. For example, what if you argued that Christian theology is actually more like creative writing, studio art, or performance?
>
> **Exercise:** Make a list of all the forms of Christian teaching presented in the theological texts you teach. How many of them do you tend to omit when planning classes? How many of them embarrass you? Why exactly?
>
> **A possible corollary:** Conforming theological education to prevailing university models encourages us to forget some powerful means for teaching theology. Forgetting them, we also forget how to recognize them as we read or write. Remembering them, we may come to regret some of what we have been teaching as theology. A change of teaching forms requires that "contents" be examined again.

Recalling Other Ways to Teach

One pervasive effect of Schleiermacher's model—or, to be fair, its descendants—is the assumption of a divide between theory and practice. This assumption contradicts many traditional Christian pedagogies. (For example, if we want to distinguish a "practical theology," what do we posit as the contrasting term? *Impractical* theology?) The version of the divide that most concerns me here is one between textual interpretation and bodily training. It is the assumption—sometimes the claim—that complicated texts play no strong role in shaping bodies. This assumption denies the power of a *textual* revelation—not to speak of inherited liturgies, lyrics in hymnody, rules of life, or devotional poetry. What is more troubling for me, it denies the experience of generations of Christians who have placed their hopes in remembered words.

Most of the teaching of Christian tradition reaches us now through texts. They act on us. The best of them make room for active response, for what cannot be fully said but only ever pursued. To call out embodied response, to elicit the action of whole persons, Christian authors have experimented with a range of forms, adapting some, inventing others. The loss during recent centuries of a full range of genres and styles in theological writing may be a greater threat to Christian teaching than institutional contraction. We ought to be concerned that Christian schools are closing. We ought to be more concerned that Christian languages shrivel up or dissipate in 24/7 distraction by a blend of information and advertising.

If we forget strong means of Christian teaching, we cannot forget needing them. The unmet need for teaching is one motive for our religious "mobility." For example, many people who leave Christianity for one or another American Buddhism report that they are drawn by spiritual instruction that is less dogmatic, less institutional, and more practical. I do not disagree. I practice an eclectic form of sitting meditation myself. I suspect that I am drawn to it because it is alluringly embedded in subtle scenes of instruction. Some American Buddhist communities now appear to be more thoughtful than many Christian churches about the variety of ways to teach.

How did that come to pass? Christians spent centuries developing nuanced practices of spiritual formation in communities of many kinds. There are easily as many lineages of transmission in Christianity as in Buddhism, each with its models and records of teaching. How can Christians have forgotten them? A church historian—or sociologist of religion—could multiply answers to that question while reformulating it more precisely. In this book, I hope only to pursue one response (which is not an answer), because I am less concerned with causes than with effects and remedies. I believe that many Christians have forgotten the most persuasive ways in which theology has been taught and written. They have lost the Word's beauties.

I want to recover some of those ways as inspirations for inventing more of them. I also hope to resist the erasure of the gifts of teaching and teachers. Strong pedagogy is not intrinsically abusive. If teachers need students' trust to teach deeply, they need to earn it in the students' experience of learning. A teacher gains appropriate authority as an ally to the student's desire to learn. Can that authority be abused? Of course—sometimes with horrifying consequences. But not all abuse in teaching is sexual or financial. Giving up on teaching is also an abuse of students—with damaging consequences in many spheres, especially the political.

This book offers antidotes to our growing amnesia about how teaching books can change bodily lives appropriately. It responds to the hunger for teaching relations that are powerful without being abusive. It restages old scenes of transformation, and stages new ones, as models and provocations for our teaching and writing into the future. It reopens Schleiermacher's question of whether theology should be in universities in order to pose another: If not in universities or seminaries that copy them, where *could* theological teaching find a home?

The ongoing exercise of this book is to find or make new shelters for teaching theology. I consider that the most urgent preparation for theology's future. If we save all the seminary endowments but forget teaching, we will have given up a pearl of great price and astonishing beauty.

2

Recognizing Scenes of Instruction

The Gospels included in the New Testament tell stories about a teacher. Recounted by at least four voices, the stories weave together and pull apart. The character named "Jesus" is not the same teacher in the four Gospels or in all episodes of a single one of them. Still, the stories that were made canonical agree on some important things about him.

Jesus wrote nothing. Christians affirm that, of course, but often fail to draw out implications or imitate the reserve. They suspend that part of Jesus's example. (Paul chose to write letters against his Lord's example—more confidently, perhaps, because he had never watched him teach in the flesh.) In the canonical Gospels, the only mention of Jesus writing is in the story about the woman taken in adultery (John 8:3–11). As the crowd prepares to stone her in compliance with the prescription of Leviticus 20:10, Jesus crouches down to trace words (we don't know which) "on the earth."[1] The composed scene remains evasive about writing, refusing to record even his scribbles. Jesus entrusts the shape of his teaching not to a text but to living memories of what he says and does. In his confidence, or his love, he leaves it to others to make their written records—and to make them differently. He neither practices nor prescribes writing.

Jesus is also not remembered as having spent much time with accredited teachers. Luke tells a story about his parents finding him "in the temple, sitting among the teachers (*didaskalōi*), listening to them and asking them questions" (Luke 2:46). Matthew, Mark, and Luke report that Jesus taught in a number of synagogues, though the crowds came rather for his healing. His teaching didn't always go well. In one of the most detailed scenes (Luke 4:16–30), Jesus is driven out by the enraged congregation, who then attempt to kill him. He escapes. (Should there be a question about that on our mandated evaluations? "Did you feel a desire to murder the instructor? 5: During every class session. 4: At least once a week . . .") The greater scenes of Jesus's teaching are set in houses; on lakeshores and in boats; in gardens, streets, or roads; in the open desert; and (fatally) in Jerusalem's public and private places—a borrowed room, a barracks, another garden, a hilltop used for executions. There were classrooms in that city. Jesus did not use them.

Jesus's oral instruction, delivered in a brief public life, is remembered as vivid and plainspoken but also disconcerting and enigmatic. He often baffled those who knew him best. If Jesus left his students neither code nor system, he did exhort them to remember other things. On the night before he died, at the last gathering of his movable school, he pronounced an explicit command to remember him by repeating the improvisation of a ritual. Christians often refer to the "great commandment" as the command of love (Matt. 22:35–40; Mark 12:28–34). Still, for most of the recorded memories, his *last* teaching to his students was about a table ritual. He asks them to repeat or restage a performed scene of instruction.

In a community that receives the canonical Gospels as authoritative records, stories about Jesus as teacher become models for Christian instruction. His deeds include unique signs and wonders, but also a ritual that wants to be remembered by repetition. (Jesus's teaching does not stay in the past.) He commends prayer by example as a means of ongoing discernment; he promises to send a Spirit as advocate and instructor. Each of these elements is then entrusted to texts by other authors who hope for reenactment. However exactly Christians understand the authorship of the canonical Gospels, they take them as extensions or instruments of Jesus's teaching. The teachings (*logoi*) spoken by Jesus become the words (*logoi*) of written texts. Recalling so many kinds of instruction, the texts then stage scenes of instruction in their own right. Their composition assumes the powerful interaction of texts and bodies, words and practices. In John, Jesus promises that the advocate yet to come "will teach you all things and remind you of all that I have *said* to you" (John 14:26). The Spirit teaches bodies with and without words—just as the Teacher did.

Jesus's teaching is transformed into tradition when it is remembered as repeatable scenes of instruction that often involve speech. How were the scenes shaped for transmission? There are obvious parallels between the way that Jesus taught and the teaching of other rabbis, before and after him. Rabbinic lore provided patterns. Equally important to the construction of Christian traditions were models of ancient philosophical teaching around the Mediterranean. Christian teachers had to compete against philosophers as they moved out of the Israelite homeland or scattered Jewish communities. Early Christians dissented loudly from a number of philosophical precepts, but they borrowed from their rivals' ways of staging teaching that meant to change lives.

Philosophical Scenes

In ancient philosophical writing, a scene of instruction typically needs a *place*, whether real or imagined.[2] By itself, the place addresses important questions: Is the teaching public or private? If private, what is the condition or preparation for admission? And where exactly is the entrance? How does the scene connect to the sites of daily life—the kitchen or bedroom or bath, the marketplace, the temple? A scene of instruction also needs a *time*. The teaching begins at a specified hour, answers to a season, falls on a significant holiday. Other philosophical scenes refuse to settle on the calendar. They unroll outside of time or roll time back over itself. Every scene of instruction, even one that happens in a visionary moment, takes the time required for its sequence, its steps or stages. How much time will the scene's pedagogy consume—fifty minutes, a year of late adolescence, more than a lifetime? What must happen before the scene can begin? What new futures does it prepare?

Together, place and time open space for a scene's *characters*. Characters in ancient philosophic teaching are more stylized and diverse than human beings. They do not always possess bodies, though disembodied characters—souls, virtues, laws, deities— are often lent bodies for the scene's duration. A character's body may figure a lesson or act it out. It can change, resist, suffer, fail. Characters also have souls—to use the old word. They explore patterns of thought or suffer passions; they put on virtues and shuck off vices—or the reverse. Some characters stand in for fixed qualities, but there can be no scene of instruction unless at least one character can change in soul and body. Change of character is a scene's chief action and end.

The various characters in a scene of philosophic instruction are not gaudy drapery for lessons taught more accurately as abstract rules or theories. Characters are indispensable for the kind of teaching that scenes of instruction intend. If characters exemplify certain actions, they *teach* action through the affective relations they can enable for a learner. The function of the scene is to establish and cultivate the relations through which transformative teaching takes place. A learner may feel connected to many figures in a scene, but decisive relations typically run to the scene's figuration of the teacher.

Local authorities tend to notice a teacher who has the power to change a character's shape. After all, they typically insist on delivering the final verdict about character changes in those subject to them. A teacher who exerts power attracts it. This points us to the final constituent in scenes of philosophic instruction, which is (not coincidentally) harder to name than the others. Philosophic scenes keep watch over the power flows that both sustain and constrain them. The city is the frame of political power, in the broadest sense, and so also of the ordinary uses of education for political ends. It has its prominent schools and its well-paid teachers. A scene of philosophic instruction often relies on the city's education when subverting it. Those who listen to Socrates already have their grammar and geometry, their music and gymnastics—which they learned in Athens. He attempts a risky reeducation to prepare citizen-students for membership in another kind of community.

Ancient scenes of philosophic instruction negotiate the paradoxes and politics of philosophic teaching. Some texts treat them explicitly. Plato's *Meno* begins with the question: Can virtue be taught? The person who poses it—Meno himself—doesn't understand what he asks, but glories in his verbal dexterity around a trendy topic. Socrates leads him to the possibility of learning by combining myth with practical demonstration. The reader's own anxieties about teaching are addressed in watching how Socrates can and cannot teach Meno. The anxieties find their first resolution—so far as they have one—in the dialogue's action. If Socrates fails in teaching Meno, he can still succeed in teaching a more attentive observer—the reader. Of course, the risks remain. The dialogue ends when a third character, Anytus, warns Socrates to beware powerful enemies. Paradoxes of teaching may be temporarily resolved for Meno, and an observer lured toward more lasting transformation, but the local bullies have only gotten more irritated. They want to co-opt Socrates's powers—or eliminate them by ridding themselves of him. They did.

I have talked as if these philosophic scenes happened right before our eyes. Some of them do—or once did. Much philosophical instruction in antiquity was carried out in "real time," on living bodies. A teacher would address a crowd of students or give private counsel to someone seeking care. Still, and early on, embodied scenes of instruction were doubled in written scenes. A teacher might become famous enough to merit the circulation of transcripts. Or a passionate and gifted student might forgo writing dramas to record the acts of a master who died too soon (a story told of Plato). Or a teacher-poet might choose to present scenes that could *only* be written: episodes of divine instruction in a mythic or visionary past. Once scenes are retold or represented in texts, another set of characters appears. To the characters *within* the textual frame are added the characters *of* the frame: the author and reader, the dramatist and viewer.

Writing scenes brings new risks. Some philosophic authors express sharp doubts about the texts they produce—as Plato does in both *Phaedrus* and the (so-called) seventh letter. Their doubts do not keep them from writing. Few ancient schools are reported to have refused writing altogether (though some held back choice secrets). Even teachers who disdain fancy verbal forms to emphasize bodily action encourage the circulation of illustrative stories. At the same time, few ancient writers presume that the representation of a scene of instruction is complete. At best, it offers a script or set of directions that only makes effective sense when performed.

Representation does not capture philosophical instruction so much as incite or reactivate it. Texts need bodies and souls in which to reach their conclusions—and to keep up with changing forms of life. Reactivating scenes of instruction changes them. It might even be said to instruct them about what is happening now with human learning or lives.[3]

A scene of instruction is a ritual occasion for rejuvenating language. New speakers learn an older language. They use it to address unexpected questions or situations, stretch or add vocabularies, innovate argumentative and rhetorical forms. Most of all, they revivify the inert tokens of words—forgotten, clichéd— by allowing them to shape their lives.

Christian Scenes

We inherit too many stories about the contest between ancient philosophy and Christianity, beginning, of course, with the stories that Christian polemicists tell. Sometimes their stories vituperate the older learning as the addictive poison of idolatry, which spawns monstrous hallucinations and then real vices.

Opening his exhortation to learning, Clement of Alexandria confines the raving pagan poets, with their mad fans and chorus of demons, to the art colonies of ancient myth. He points instead toward heavenly Truth enthroned upon Mount Zion as "the true contender crowned on the stage before the whole cosmos" (*Protreptikos* 1.3). However fiercely Clement casts out the older literature, its corrupting manners, its vain wisdom, he borrows from its style and its pedagogy. He rewrites learned allegory to attack empty learning. He borrows both arguments and genre from philosophic texts written long before the Gospels. I called Clement's work an exhortation, but that is a dilute translation for *protreptikos*. Aristotle devotes the influential work *Protreptic* to the study of philosophy. He moves from the common accusation that studying philosophy is deadly to the conclusion that you might as well give up living if you refuse to study philosophy. A Latin imitation of Aristotle's *Protreptic*, Cicero's *Hortensius*, opened the ears of the young Augustine to a call from beyond the clanging of the market in alluring bodies (*Confessions* 3.4.7). Later in *Confessions*, through his protracted wrestling with some Platonic books, Augustine lays out ways in which the highest pagan philosophy falls short of the Gospel truths (7.9.13–15). Of course, even as he claims that Christianity is the more powerful and inventive teacher, Augustine risks conceding how much it learned from its predecessor.

Successors in so many ways to ancient teachers of philosophy, early Christians regularly write with the confidence that written scenes can produce decisive effects. The highest example is Christian trust in the teaching power of *Scriptures*. To receive Scriptures is to trust that writing can aid divine salvation. (This trust is not inevitable. It is easy to imagine that Jesus's refusal to write could have become a community prohibition against the production of new scriptures. That kind of Christianity might have been less eager to convert empires.) Once written down, Jesus's scenes begin to produce effects through features peculiar to writing. Consider Matthew's telling of the Sermon on the Mount (chaps. 5–7). Whatever we might wish for *lectio divina*, reading Matthew is not exactly the same as hearing Jesus. Nor is the gospel text only a script for reciting an oral teaching, as if from memory. The written scene depends on textual devices of allusion and symmetry, abbreviated description, deliberate omission. It displays a variety of characters, but it also invites new relations from a reader to Jesus through the narrator. As an *inherited* text, the Sermon on the Mount also encourages a reader to enter into relations with earlier communities that transmitted it, interpreting it all the while.

I underline this point because it is easy to miss. The written Gospels tell us that Jesus used many ways to teach other than writing. He preached enigmas that stuck in memory. He performed actions of mercy, including healing miracles. He called those he encountered to join him on the road. Jesus denounced religious and political powers. He urged the repetition of a specific table ritual. He suffered before dying courageously. According to his intimate friends, he then rose from the dead—whatever exactly that means. We now learn these things in many ways—by hearing the stories, by repeating the ritual. Still, we mainly read about Jesus's teaching in texts—even though the texts do not record him ordering or encouraging his students to write. The self-conscious author of Luke-Acts claims as his motive a desire to arrange in a proper digest what has been handed down by original attendants of the oral teaching. There is no appeal to a divine command: the author says only, "it seemed good also *to me*" to write in order to provide the "certainty" or "security" of those teachings (Luke 1:1–4). Consider this countercaution at the end of John: Jesus did many more things than have ever been written about. If you tried to record them singly, it is unlikely that "the whole cosmos could contain the books written" (John 21:25). Writing is still a question for our evangelists.

If written scenes of instruction are everywhere in Christian tradition, why draw attention to them? The compromises required to get theology into universities and keep it there have often sacrificed its characteristic ways of teaching. That is notably the case now, under the model we attribute to Schleiermacher. I pay attention to the occluded scenes in the hope of gaining back the practices. There is no better way to do that than by reactivating the scenes played through us by influential Christian texts. Easier said than done. Academic exegesis often reduces the Gospels and other narratives of Christian teaching to their hypothesized stages of composition, inferred social milieus, implicit ideologies, and so on. All those descriptions run aslant of the teaching drama that the text is designed to assist. The same can happen with the notion of theological "tradition." It changes from a living transmission to a code of law subject to forensic debate and authoritative determination. More recently, more poignantly, the teaching of Christian texts can be refused out of "political" concerns attached to the presumed social "identities" of their authors. I agree that we should ask—even suspiciously— who exactly is teaching through a text. We should also discern whether our well-being requires that we set aside a particular text at a given moment. Still, none of that should prevent us from engaging the variety of transformative teaching in Christian texts— once we consent to enter into them.

When I talk about "entering" a scene, I use a simple physical metaphor for the half-hidden processes by which texts "come to life" (another metaphor) in our minds and bodies. Even my more abstract talk of "reactivating" a scene is metaphorical or analogous. To replace the metaphor of reactivation with a more "literal" or more detailed analysis would require a long digression. That digression wouldn't help here. But perhaps I can say a bit more about what the metaphor of reactivation does and does not imply. I use it to name reading practices that restore the powers of persuasion to a text. Finding effective meaning in an old text, you do more than repeat its words. You gather new words to reperform its persuasion in the changed languages and historical circumstances of your present. More robust remaking is required to inherit ethical texts. If I want to read an ancient ethical handbook well, I need to handle its concepts, arguments, and narratives nimbly enough to reuse them. I must also develop some lively sense of how its precepts for cases or its patterns for ways of life might be acted out in my present. Most of all, I must appreciate and perhaps imitate the sound of the voice that makes precepts or patterns ethically attractive, persuasive in the more sustained way that ethics requires.

I repeat: a scene of instruction is a ritual occasion for revivifying language. Language comes alive not as testable memorization but as living speech. The authority of the scene is secured or confirmed in what new speakers can do with their new tongues—and how that capacity answers to the desires that impelled their learning. The multiplication of languages at Pentecost is about not only translation but also transmission across time. Babel is the historical backdrop for teaching any tradition. Teaching theology requires a gift of tongues.

An example may help. Thomas Aquinas's *Summa theologiae* is one of the most widely taught and commented upon texts of Christian theology. It has been translated into many languages—beginning, early on, with Byzantine Greek. (What was it like to hear Aristotle coming back into latter-day Greek through medieval Latin?) The *Summa* has also been explained in many languages while being taught to generations of students around the globe. Regular classroom exposition of Thomas justified ongoing scholarship at advanced levels. His works were not only edited and republished according to changing tastes, they were defended against evolving philosophies, sciences, and theologies. The result? There emerged so many Thomisms—never singular, always plural—that sorting them became its own specialty. Within the quarreling lineages, teaching the *Summa* means choosing its meanings—for a particular context, of course, but also against rival readings.

What is more important—reactivating Thomas's text requires revivifying it inwardly. Someone who understands the five "ways" to God (misnamed as proofs) must be able to perform the meditations that Thomas's text lays out. She must do more. To understand the five ways in *Summa* 1.3.3 is to pay new attention to the grounding insight conveyed through the text. A reader is invited to perform the kind of reasoning Thomas proposes in her present—not in some fantasy of Thomas's past. (Fantasies of theology's haloed past too easily become policies for church police in the present.) She must be able to speak or write Thomas again, in the currently available languages and styles of embodiment. Reactivating is remaking. If it is well constructed, a scene of instruction will dispose its place, time, and characters to aid in its own re-creation. Still, a scene cannot determine the unpredictable reiteration of its own insights, images, arguments, and possibilities. It could not do that even in the first instance.

Activating a Christian scene, a reader encounters its characteristic paradoxes. The root paradoxes of Christian teaching arise from grace. Augustine devotes a treatise to refuting the clever objection that church members should not be scolded since they can do good only if given divine assistance. Instead of harassing their congregants, so the objection goes, church leaders would do better to beseech God for an outpouring of help (*On Rebuke and Grace* 2.4–4.6). In another book, after elaborate analyses of scriptural interpretation and artful preaching, Augustine writes: "Even with the ministry of holy people, or the interventions of holy angels, no one rightly learns the lessons about living with God unless God makes them teachable *by* God. . . . The helps of teaching that human beings offer can reach the soul only when God causes them to reach it—God, who can give the Gospel to us without us and without going through us" (*On Christian Teaching* 4.16.33).

This paradox of teaching precedes Augustine, of course. Jesus is remembered to have said, "You are not to be called 'Rabbi,' for you have one teacher (*didaskalos*)" (Matt. 23:8). If there is only one (divine) Christian teacher, what are Christians doing when they "teach"? Can they do more than gesture toward the prior teaching of Jesus? Or do they participate in his teaching, somehow "channeling" it? But many early lists of indispensable Christian ministries include teachers (*didaskaloi*)—though not, of course, "theologians" (1 Cor. 12:28–29; Eph. 4:11; James 3:1). (The Greek and Latin antecedents of our word "theology" were pagan terms before they were Christian. Given Augustine's polemic against the pagan uses, centuries passed before Western Christians began to apply the word to their own teaching.)

Other paradoxes arise in Jesus's saying about the title "teacher." For example, if one assumes that the "one teacher" is Jesus or the one Jesus called "Father," then Christian teaching must occur as much by deed as by word. Jesus's deeds include not only speeches and acts of mercy but also suffering unto death. If Christian teaching requires suffering and resurrection, life after death, how should human teachers proceed? Do they teach in order to be martyred? Martyred how? (Bonhoeffer: "Every call of Christ leads into death.")[4] Again, Jesus's teaching is often the opposite of clear. He knots language. He whispers at the border of silence. He preaches suspicion of any worldly wisdom. A few stories about Jesus's childhood make him a prodigy, but there are no stories about his receiving a first-class education at an elite institution. Paul, who was better educated, recognized the implication: "If anyone among you considers himself wise (*sophos*) in this age, let him [her, them] become foolish so that he might become wise. For the wisdom (*sophia*) of this world is foolishness according to God" (1 Cor. 3:18–19). Yet Paul continues to teach even as he denounces the pretenses of worldly learning. His scenes of instruction negotiate their own dependency on the essential teaching, which is divine.

Within a Christian scene, a learner will inevitably also encounter the difficulties of politics and power. These are most evident in what I call policing. The policing of Christian scenes is notably more violent than that in schools of ancient philosophy. The Pythagoreans were notorious for the severity of their discipline and demands for secrecy, but Pythagorean mythology leaves punishment to the gods. Christians have been less reticent about acting on God's behalf to enforce (their) orthodoxies. Among the "pedagogies" authorized by saintly example, a reader can find merciless polemic, silencing, exclusion (as figure of damnation), physical abuse, and execution. To the evangelical paradoxes of any Christian teaching, church history has added the contradictions of coercion.

Paradoxes and policing are negotiated in actual scenes. So, too, is teaching. A teaching text enables performances of learning. These must be *done*, not described or recollected at a comfortable distance. Of course, human doing should always proceed under cautions about its limits. In any theology classroom, a human being is never the most important teacher. There are at least two others, of unequal importance. There is the inherited text, the shape of which carries potencies for soul shaping. There is God, without whom no efficacious teaching of theology can proceed. Ben Lerner writes of poetry: "What kind of art is defined—has been defined for millennia by such a rhythm of denunciation and defense?" He adds, "Poetry isn't hard, it's impossible." And again, "There is no genuine poetry: there is only, after all, at best, a place for it."[5] We can apply each of those remarks with greater strictness to the poetry called Christian theology. Teaching Christian theology isn't hard, it's impossible—for human beings.

> **Exercise**: Describe in not fewer than one thousand words how Christian teaching would proceed if it had never encountered Greco-Roman philosophy. (Hint: This may be a trick question, not least because the required length is too *long*. Try removing the minimum word count. Then let yourself write anything, including sentences like "The terms can't move that way" or "That feels like a nonsense question.")
>
> **Exercise**: In class, how do you draw attention to the paradoxical limits in your teaching of theology? Setting aside the words you use, describe your facial expressions, gestures, inarticulate sounds, and silences. What do they convey? Would they convey your sense better or worse if you performed them more often? Or punctuated your teaching with lengthening silences? And when you begin to *write* theology, how do you translate such expressions, gestures, sounds, silences into text?

1

BODIES

Gregory of Nyssa, Life of Macrina

Around the middle of his earthly life, a teacher was consecrated bishop at the urging of his brother, who was already renowned for skill in church leadership. The man's appointment was immediately controversial. He had to confront many of the ways that civil politics can dominate—can deform—Christian life. Seven years further on, the man's brother and sister died in quick succession. She too was a famous leader, most immediately of a community of women. He was squeezed hard by grief. After several more years, he was moved to write about his sister's death. Someone he met on pilgrimage had heard about the remarkable woman and wanted to learn more, especially from an intimate witness. In response, the man began to write a letter—though his text quickly sprawled beyond any letter's limits. It became an open-ended testimony to how his sister taught.[1]

The letter traces the ways in which Christ's teaching takes flesh in human bodies. It rehearses old philosophical problems of bodily life, especially the control of unruly desires and destructive passions. Then it shows how incarnation runs through human lives that are shaped by Scripture, liturgy, and community. It makes clear that an ongoing education of the body is required in church leaders. Our author is a bishop who has come to his dying sister for lessons about the griefs that seize his body, shedding its tears.

How Not to Reactivate Texts

You may already have recognized the story I'm telling. The man was Gregory of Nyssa. His distinguished siblings were Basil of Caesarea, also a bishop, and Macrina, the renowned head of a community of holy women. The pilgrim who spurred him to write was a monk named Olympius. They met on a trip to Jerusalem "to see in those places the signs of the Lord's coming into flesh" (no. 1). Gregory was visiting the places where Jesus taught through flesh when he was asked to tell about another bodily teaching he had witnessed.

My aim in retelling Gregory's *Life of Macrina* is to reactivate its nested scenes of incarnate instruction. I hope to help its words change from artifacts into living speech. To do that, I began to tell it as a *story* worth hearing in its own right—a story that you might be eager to follow without worrying first about historical "contexts" and scholarly "sources." I omitted elements that are now standard when teaching old texts in university or seminary classrooms. Seeing my chapter title, you would not have been surprised if I had started like this: "Gregory of Nyssa (ca. 335–ca. 395) was a Christian theologian and church leader who, with Basil of Caesarea (his brother) and Gregory of Nazianzus, formed the eminent trio known as the 'Cappadocian Fathers.' Long influential in Eastern Christian churches, he has gained new prominence among Western Christians in the last hundred years." You might have been bored by that recital, but it would not have surprised you. That sort of introduction is tediously familiar. Unfortunately, it frustrates a reader's access to a scene of instruction—and not just by tedium.

Consider the parenthetical dates. They suggest that an author like Gregory, having lived a long time ago, can be understood only within his historical period or place. The dates remove Gregory from the present and place him at a distance on the agreed map of history. Now, I am the last person to ignore contrasts between long-ago writers and present-day readers. I consider them so important that I want to attend to all of them, including disagreements about history, both as time and as story. Over centuries, Christian writers have espoused very different notions about their relations to history. Assuming Gregory's historical otherness—assuming that he is confined to his time as we are to ours—contradicts what he and many Christians have claimed for living tradition. According to them, when you become a Christian, you join a community that bends history in unexpected ways. (That is one meaning of the phrase "the communion of saints.") Believers are linked across time and outside of time. The past continues in the present. Indeed, the past was enacted with the present in mind.

I acknowledge the arrogant risks of supersession in these claims. The antidote, so far as there is one, is to admit ignorance of what the claims might mean for other divine pedagogies. If I assert that the Law was given to Moses partly for me as a Christian, I can in the next moment confess that God might also have given it to Moses for purposes that I cannot recognize, much less comprehend. However we restate it, the claim of living tradition has been a fundamental conviction in much scriptural exegesis. It remains the disconcerting confidence of sacramental and liturgical traditions. (For some Christians, the Last Supper is both cited and repeated at every Eucharist. Others sing at the Easter vigil, "*This* is the night in which you led our parents, the children of Israel, out of Egypt and across the Red Sea, safely dry.") The claim of access through time issues from the more outrageous claim that God became incarnate once to reach all peoples. To read Gregory from within such a tradition is to trust that his old text may indeed become present again as living teaching. Inserting distancing dates after the names of great theologians can distract from reading them as theologians.

The standard introduction to someone like Gregory raises other obstacles, which I'll mention only in passing. For example, the label "Cappadocian Fathers" belongs not to Gregory's authorship but to later classifications of it. It may suggest that everything important in his varied books can be summarized by an intellectual label that he shares with two other writers. That sort of summary is grossly unfair—both to writers and readers. (People some-times define poetry as untranslatable. For me, any philosophy or theology worth reading cannot be summarized.) Another obstacle put up by the standard introduction to Gregory is the unqualified claim that he was "a theologian" and "church leader." That label-ing skips over questions about how he actually described himself or what he took to be the task of teaching in relation to commu-nity leadership. It also suggests that roles like "theologian" and "church leader" don't change. They do. If all believers are linked in some way across history, they still lie under the curse of Babel: they speak opposed languages that change daily.

My point should be clear even if it is not persuasive. When you mean to enter Gregory's scene of instruction, you must set aside such standard introductions. *Tolle, lege.* Pick him up and read (to appropriate Augustine, *Confessions* 8.12).

Macrina's Pattern of Life

A Christian teacher has been asked to tell what he learned from his sister, not least in her death. Who was she?

Gregory first describes Macrina as someone who "raised her-self by philosophy to the greatest height of human virtue" (no. 1). "Philosophy" for Gregory is not the sort of logical analysis taught in many English-speaking universities. It is rather the opposite. By "philosophy" Gregory means the pursuit of a vision that directs you toward your highest end, which is the fullest actualization of what you are. Choosing this word, Gregory calls forward the many schools of ancient philosophy founded before Christ's incarna-tion. He engages particularly their patterns for dying well. The philosophical model directly in front of him is Plato's *Phaedo.* That dialogue retells Socrates's last day, at the end of which he was executed by the city of Athens on trumped-up charges. (West-ern philosophy, like Christianity, takes as its founding deed a po-litical execution.) The memory of that death, handed down from one student to another, renews the call to practice philosophy while alive. For Gregory, the memory of Macrina's life and death matches this Platonic example only to exceed it. Like Socrates, Macrina spends her last mortal hours discoursing on the soul: "she philosophized for us about the soul, explaining the cause of life in flesh, why a human being exists, how it became mortal and where death arose, and which is the liberation from this to another life" (no. 18). Those are Socrates's topics exactly, but Gregory puts the details of Macrina's lectures from that day into a separate work, *On the Soul and Resurrection*. What Plato keeps together in the *Phaedo*, Gregory separates. Macrina has more incisive teaching to give than arguments. (Of course, the same could be said of Plato's Socrates. Just before the end of the *Phaedo*, he leaves his students a myth and an example of courage under tyranny.)

Telling a life has been a privileged genre for Christian writing. Hagiography is not an incidental Christian form. It honors the Gospels by imitating them. Christians are led through one or another saintly life back to Jesus's pattern. Gregory reminds his readers at many points, explicitly and implicitly, that Macrina reflects the life of Christ. Indeed, the text alerts us that it could tell much more about her "healing diseases, casting out demons, true predictions of things to come" (no. 39). Gregory quotes a soldier who exclaims that the cures Macrina accomplished by faith were only a little less wondrous than the Lord's own. Jesus's life keeps appearing through hers as source and goal.

Jesus's life and his words: Christian Scripture is the deep bass underneath Macrina's speech—her prayers, certainly, but also her instruction and conversation. Might Gregory have adjusted biographical details and remembered conversations in order to amplify the scriptural notes? Of course! Instead of regarding that as deception, we might consider it discernment. To see a life as Christian means recognizing Christ through it; to retell a life as Christian is to emphasize its gospel murmurings. For Gregory, a holy life is a scriptural life. It is also liturgical, since liturgy is a graced reperformance of the scriptural history of salvation. (Among other things, the "public work," the *leitourgia*, is giving soul and body to recapitulations of the divine drama.) Dying, Macrina enacts Scriptures as narrative and sacrament.

Gregory's Bodily Education

According to Gregory, telling Macrina's life as Christian cannot exclude telling it as philosophical. Her teaching gathers whatever truths philosophers discovered to complete them. She can do this in part because she hopes for the redemption of bodies.

Among the nested scenes of instruction, the most vivid is Macrina's room during the hours before and after her death. The room recalls and then replaces the site of an Athenian execution described by Plato. Socrates was a teacher who could turn a jail into a school for meeting death without weeping. Macrina's teaching is more powerful still. She hurries toward death with the anticipation of a bride at her wedding because she can see Jesus waiting just on the other side.

In this text, Macrina's main student is Gregory himself. He must be taught by careful steps how to confront his own unruly grief. When Gregory is dejected by the mention of his dead brother, Macrina turns their conversation to "stronger philosophy" and offers a discourse on the immortal soul (no. 18). When Gregory laments his own troubles as bishop, she scolds him for not recognizing God's gifts. Macrina teaches him finally—decisively—by her encounter with death. As the rest of the community rushes into the room weeping (performing again the grief of Socrates's students), Gregory joins them. His tears rehearse Phaedo's own. Then Gregory regains composure. He rebukes the weepers by recalling Macrina's bodily example. Even the marks on her body confirm the lessons of Christian poverty, asceticism, and trust in God. The scene of explicit instruction by word and deed is carried beyond death by her now mute body. Imitating Jesus in this last way, her body too becomes a scene of instruction. "Take your hand and put it into my side, and do not be untrusting but trusting" (John 20:27).

After Macrina's death, Gregory wants to cover her corpse in sumptuous funeral wrappings. There are none to be had. Macrina had commanded that no fancy clothes be bought in preparation. She also ordered that Gregory tend to her body with his own hands. This command suspends ordinary decencies—and allows him to discover, while cleaning and dressing her corpse, some records of her education by God. The suspension of decency lasts only as long as the teaching scene. By the time Gregory goes to bury Macrina in the family grave, he is afraid of violating his parents' dignity by seeing them unclothed and decayed. The transparency of Macrina's body to the body of Jesus is only a flicker, not steady resurrection light. That is yet to come—for Macrina herself and for her generations of students.

The Surrounding Scenes

If Macrina's room is Gregory's central stage of instruction, others are narrated, others still mentioned.

Gregory reviews Macrina's education, beginning in childhood. She is not raised on literature (in our sense), because it would excite tragic passions. Much less is she exposed to indecent comedy. Macrina is tutored instead by portions of Scripture that carry her toward an ethical life. She also recites the Psalms, turning daily duties toward liturgy while committing to memory patterns of feeling.

Another set of scenes depicts the variety of people that Macrina teaches. There is Basil, her brother (and Gregory's), who returns puffed up from success at school. Macrina deflates him so that he will relinquish vanity for philosophy. Next is their youngest brother, Peter, to whom she serves as "father, teacher (*didaskalos*), tutor (*paidagōgos*), mother, adviser of all good" (no. 12). Finally, Macrina teaches her own mother, reminding her at another family death to rebuke the ills of passion with reason, conquering nature by argument. Much of this sounds like pagan education in stern virtue, but Gregory points beyond what philosophy can attain. As Macrina and her mother reach the heights of philosophy, living almost as if free from death, they undertake "the meditation of divine realities, unceasing prayer, the uninterrupted singing of hymns" (no. 11).

Macrina's death, her education, her early teaching: around these scenes are others in which Gregory, schooled by Macrina, takes the role of teacher. His students include the monk, Olympius, who first heard the holy woman's story and asked that it be written down. Once finished, the text will find many other students. Gregory has them already in view, since he limits his narrative for fear of misleading "fleshly" beginners in faith. Gregory must be thinking not of Olympius but of other, later readers. If they—if we—may not yet hear of Macrina's miracles, they can and should read the scene of her death and burial. They may witness her better-than-Socratic teaching and her more-than-Socratic joy at the approach of Jesus. They too can read the lessons left on her body.

For Gregory's text to accomplish any of this, it must respond to its students' desires. That is not to say that it must satisfy or even endorse students' immediate articulations of what they currently want. It may be that Olympius asked Gregory to give more information about Macrina for the best of motives. It is more likely that the motives were mixed: love of God, sober piety, but perhaps also an itch for astonishing news or eagerness to champion a new saint. Gregory's text must sustain the mixture of motives long enough to redirect them—that is, to educate them. Serious learning requires strong motives. Serious teaching often needs to lure motives in other directions without diluting them.

I pause the retelling of Gregory's scenes there. You must have some doubts about them. Certainly I do. Still, there is no need to judge an account as "all true" in order to learn something from it. (Christian theology is written and read by sinners.) A scene may work on its readers by leading them to wonder how much of it is true in which ways. It may raise the acute question, "Whom should I trust here—and how far?"

A scene can teach without asserting itself as the only scene. For Gregory it would be blasphemous for anyone to receive his text as more than a stammering paraphrase of better teaching in the Gospels.

4

Marcella Althaus-Reid,
Indecent Theology

Marcella Althaus-Reid provoked embarrassment on the way to theology. Among readers of her *Indecent Theology*, for example, you can produce blushes by repeating four words: "lemon vendors without underwear."[1] Or just hold up the book's cover. (If you don't recall the front of the 2000 edition published by Routledge, search for it online now. Compare the cover photograph on the 2005 Spanish version by Bellaterra.) Althaus-Reid never squandered her readers' embarrassment. She raised it up into scenes of instruction.

Althaus-Reid was magnificently attuned to the social identities that the English-speaking academy imposed on her to salve its embarrassments. She was assigned the role of the fiery *Latina*, raised in the slums of Buenos Aires, who had somehow managed to escape. Her assigned task: to fuse liberation theology with sexual theology while flashing her eyes and using her polished boots for tango footwork. Her strongest theological claims might then be minimized: "You'll have to excuse her, she's . . . *foreign*. But so amusing!" Althaus-Reid laughed at these identity expectations. Then she scavenged them for her embarrassing scenes.

Learning Theology from Lemon Vendors

Consider the blushworthy beginning of *Indecent Theology*, where Althaus-Reid pretends to offer herself as a tour guide to show you, dear (Anglo) reader, some theologically significant sights in Buenos Aires, "my city" (2). An expert tour guide, she can tell you exactly where to find lemon vendors who refuse to put on underwear. She speaks of them from experience: "I know, because once I was one of them, a poor woman on the streets of Buenos Aires" (5). It's not surprising when she suggests that we take these women—or herself—as "living metaphors" useful for manufacturing new theology. That's just what the globalized economy of Christian theology expects from an Argentinian liberation theologian who's giving testimony: we expect that she'll supply us with raw material for the theological factories of Manhattan or New Haven or (either) Cambridge. Then—watch out, dear reader—instead of appropriating these women or herself as raw theological material, she diverts the tour's itinerary.

Writing theology, it turns out, is not a matter of adding new features to existing product lines. Doing that only furthers the plans of male-dominated colonial theology, which has an uncanny capacity to absorb exotic perspectives—to turn the people's markets of Buenos Aires into so many *maquiladoras* for US universities. We should seek instead "a theology [that] understands that the dislocation of sexual constructions goes hand in hand with strategies for the dislocation of hegemonic political and economic agendas" (6). To reform political power, we have to dislocate "sexual constructions," including the "idealism and romantic visions of femininity" still perpetuated by some feminisms and the squirming about sex in the best-selling liberation theology. Althaus-Reid urges us to acknowledge that theology as we have so far practiced it—even in liberation theology, even in feminist liberation theology—has been a *concealed* "sexual project." It has continued to depend "on a sexed understanding of dualistic relationships" that serves to legitimate ruling powers (7).

That's one example of Althaus-Reid undoing sexual identities and the others that flow from them. She refuses to play the fiery *Latina* Tour Guide but also the Collegial Feminist or the Liberationist-in-Unquestioning-Solidarity. If she is less explicitly critical of LGBTQIA efforts, she is still not interested in promoting queer theologies eager to enlist in prevailing identity campaigns.

None of this means to deny the painful, violent, often lethal consequences of identities assigned to bodily variations. Constructions built on assigned differences are matters of life and death. People suffer, shatter, die because of the artificial constructions stamped onto their bodies. Althaus-Reid never denies these horrors. What is just as important, she never concedes ultimate reality to their propaganda. Relying on sexual identities prevents us from acknowledging how little we yet understand about the divine creation of sex. We need to follow the confusions, slips, equivocations that identities conceal to discover how much more there is to learn about our sexes, from them, in relation with the divine.

Evading ready-made roles is an essential part of Althaus-Reid's teaching persona. Nothing can be learned from her so long as standard expectations block the way. If you know in advance the lesson Althaus-Reid has been designated to deliver, you cannot hear what she says beyond the prevailing identity scripts. If you refuse to examine your assumptions about "sex itself," refuse to doubt even for a second sex's sovereignty, then you remain trapped—whether you count yourself liberal or conservative. For Althaus-Reid, as for Plato's Socrates or Jesus of the Gospels, the doubt provoked by irony is an indispensable tool for teaching urgent things under the gaze of power.

God at the Margins

With other Christian theologians, Althaus-Reid writes sometimes of God "at the margins." More than most, she is aware of the phrase's ambiguities. The relation of center to margin is typically defined from the center. So-called margins—slums, *barrios*, *favelas*, *banlieues*, shanties, *jugghis*—are in fact centers for those who live there. But it isn't enough to replace just the terminology of center and margin. "Going to the margins" requires a deeper change in the pilgrim. Some theologians, like some tourists, pronounce confidently, in their own languages, on places they barely pass through. But if God is the God of margins, then theologians from the "center" need to *move* to the margins, to dwell there. They have to write on the margins as perpetual newcomers, preparing to meet a God who may want to remain strange because already everywhere. (Hopkins, "As Kingfishers Catch Fire": "Christ plays in ten thousand places, / Lovely in limbs, and lovely in eyes not his.")

Where are these margins? What catches this fire's light? How *do* you stage a scene of theological instruction on a margin? Althaus-Reid starts to talk about a margin only to flip locations. In *Indecent Theology*, she quotes lines from a pop song by Fito Páez: "Apocalypse from below / a sea-quake of love / party in the street / an orgasm without end / day of resurrection" (121).[2] She picks up on the song's double association of apocalypse with unsuspected resurrection: endless orgasm in the neglected streets of the *barrios* of Buenos Aires. Then Althaus-Reid's thoughts turn to Matthew Shepard, who was strung up and left to die on a buck-and-rail fence as she wrote these pages. Laramie, Wyoming, is another margin—at least, for a young gay man. Is Matthew going to resurrect? she wonders. Only if we take as our common task seeking resurrection in intimate relations. A queer bar can be a margin; so can a bedroom. God appears in both, bidden or unbidden.

Althaus-Reid imagines Jesus before the tomb of Lazarus—another sort of margin. "A man who cried as Jesus did according to the [gospel] text, and shouted to his beloved to come back from death, must have given so many kisses and cuddles to that beloved when he returned that it makes me sigh with envy just to think about it" (122). If we go to the margins to rescue unfortunate foreigners or to report on the proletarian uprising (from a sheltered balcony, of course, laptop fully charged), we may find a resurrection of our lost lovers, at least one of whom is God. Our half-ashamed loves are privileged scenes of theological instruction.

Pedagogies of Blasphemy and Obscenity

Althaus-Reid sometimes inflects theological scenes into more theatrical performances. One year, she confesses, she planned to attend Carnival as the Virgin of Guadalupe. The layers of masquerade are more complicated than might first appear. "It was an inspiration. I suddenly realized that for the next carnival in Buenos Aires I should go out as a female impersonator of the Virgin of Guadalupe" (47). You can read that as "I, a female, impersonating Guadalupe" or "I impersonating a female impersonator who is impersonating Guadalupe." The free play of bodies and costumes directs attention again to divine teaching through flesh that is too often counted only a commodity or burden. In the legend of Guadalupe, God fills the rough cloak of a colonial subject with unseasonable roses to overcome the cynicism of a colonizing archbishop. Althaus-Reid is inspired to join that scene of instruction.

However you read it, her plan may strike you as gratuitously blasphemous. Perhaps so—but then significant theological reform requires a little blasphemy. (One believer's blasphemy is another's purification. Early Calvinists despoiled churches of their images in obedience to a commandment that church artists had known for centuries but understood differently.) According to Althaus-Reid, official theology desexualizes Mary's body in feckless efforts to prevent questions about God's relation to human sex. (To argue that God *had* to become incarnate of a virgin treats ordinary procreation as an extraordinary threat.) An obvious but mistaken remedy would be to reconstruct Mary's sexuality on the assumption that we know all about sexuality and how to interpret its evidence. Althaus-Reid suggests a better way: "We do not need to speculate biblically on Mary's sexuality, but we must be ready to be that sort of reader who can understand texts sexually through our experiences: to name what is not nameable" (77). If theology has been eager to drill us in what we must say about sex, it is not so skilled in helping us to bring sexual epiphanies or transfigurations into speech. We cannot name our sexual lives because we have been schooled since childhood in their perfect regulation.

Whether choosing a carnival costume or resolving to witness the nameless, Althaus-Reid urges theological writers to enter scenes of instruction with unencumbered bodies, unruly or unclean as they might feel. For theologians who hardly know how to begin such a task, Althaus-Reid prescribes a little Christology.

Indecent Theology sketches the three exercises in Christ's obscenity. The deliberate use of obscenity as a theological method has been announced by the book's subtitle: *Theological Perversions in Sex, Gender, and Politics*. To clarify her sense, Althaus-Reid will often hyphenate: for example, "per-version," turning aside. So too, following Sartre, Althaus-Reid understands obscenity as a body's twisting visibility, a striptease. It is "the *dis-covering* of grace, and the way to transcendence" (111). Obscenity is a body's disruption of the appearance of good order in favor of grace. Since grace is the original environment for bodies, Althaus-Reid hopes that seeing Christ's body will further reveal the everywhere-margin for divine encounters.

The first "dis-covering" of grace through Christ requires us to restore sex to Jesus's body, undoing the erasure of his genitals. The point is not to savor fantasies about his sex life. It is to remove the boundary control in assumptions that Christ *must have been* "normal"—that is, heterosexual. Bi/Christ shows the graced reality of human lives beyond the currently favored identities. He is not a divine policeman clearing a path for this season's winner in the culture wars.

The second exercise in "obscenity" (always with Althaus-Reid's sense) rejects a "lust-less" Messiah in order to invite the theologian's desire back into theology. She returns to her book's beginning. Lemon vendors are not the only ones who might neglect to cover themselves. Althaus-Reid has urged that theologians too should write after slipping off undergarments. Their liberation depends in part on bodily practices. (Part of the shock readers should feel is the unexpected return of that very old claim.)

With the third "obscenity," Althaus-Reid turns from liberation to resurrection. Liberation theology has not considered resurrection well enough—for understandable reasons. It was concerned with those "disappeared" under one tyranny or another. More: liberation theology did not want to reintroduce a justification of present suffering by pointing to some future reward. But Althaus-Reid refuses to delay resurrection. She discovers its anticipations right now. For example, she finds them in the intimacy of bodies.

With this, Althaus-Reid suddenly bends back to the basic task of theology—or its possibility: "The obscene (re-discovery) of God in Indecent Theology may prove that perhaps God still exists, but for that we shall need to have a sexual-story case style of doing theology from people's sexual experiences" (124). Theology overcomes (or reverses?) the death of God when it "dis-covers" the living, sexed body of Christ. Of course, his sex is not our sex—not yet. One outcome of these exercises in obscene thinking is to show how different our sex might be from the decent versions of it. Remember, of course, that the market has its decencies—especially when it comes to representing sex. "Hot white male (gym 5X week), 20s, healthy, professional, discreet, seeks no-strings-attached play during lunch hour."

Indecent Scenes of Instruction

Many readers have found Althaus-Reid's obscenities (in her sense) to be merely obscene (in the ordinary sense). They have also found them titillating—which is no small part of the second obscenity. Closer attention to the scene of *Indecent Theology* may show how much the titillation is created by the reader.

Despite the exhortations to do theology "from people's sexual experiences," the book tells us almost nothing about its author's sex life. For Althaus-Reid, the christological "obscenities" are precisely not occasions to picture Jesus's sexual activities. (That would be just another variation on the search for the historical Jesus, who is often revealed, at last, as the searcher's imaginary friend.) Putting the idea of sex next to theology's theories of Christ detonates some of their assumptions. It undoes the metaphysics of decency—the fretful craving for purity—that animates so much theological system. ("You must be absolutely rigorous," that is, spotless.) Writing theology without underwear changes words, sensibilities, categories, narratives. It brings the writer's vulnerable, desiring body into an untidy space—call it a "margin"—where unexpected scenes of divine instruction are experienced before they are written down.

Gregory of Nyssa suffers multiple scruples about bodily decency. Althaus-Reid clearly means to undo decency—to raise questions about why a talented young woman like Macrina would find her only option to be an unmarried life with mother and the angels. But Althaus-Reid shares with Gregory and Macrina the conviction that divine lessons register through bodies. They are traced on skin. The doctrine of creation, doubled by incarnation, assigns human bodies a leading role in the divine scene of instruction. Animated by that theologian's confidence, Althaus-Reid is reserved in describing bodily lives. If God moves through our flesh, then it must glow with mystery. The worry of *Indecent Theology* is not that its readers may be "fleshy." It is that they won't be fleshy enough—that they will exchange the divine promises made to and through bodies for popular semblances of the human (compare Rom. 1:23). If you need an example, consult billboards.

Flesh might appear to be the enveloping scene for *Indecent Theology*. A reader can compile quickly enough the particular episodes in which it appears: the market of the lemon vendors, the poor living in cardboard boxes, trans sex-workers on the margins of the Pan-American Highway, Fito Páez's imagination of endless orgasm in the streets, Althaus-Reid herself impersonating a drag queen as the Virgin of Guadalupe. These scenes are indeed the ones that readers tend to remember. Still, the book's scene of instruction is at once more capacious and more familiar. It is the reader's conflicted *imagination* of flesh: disavowed desires, unspoken fantasies, clammy ideals—and, underneath, breathing and a beating heart. Althaus-Reid recommends writing theology without underwear using our own sexual lives as cases. She then refuses to strip down for us or to whisper her secrets. Her book directs us to our own writing. The teaching scene of *Indecent Theology* begins with tourists blushing. It ends when the reader's shame becomes critical reflection. For Althaus-Reid, as for Gregory, flesh lures desire to instruct it.

5

Classrooms

I have juxtaposed two Christian texts about teaching through bodies. Comparison is a familiar device in the classroom, and I have fallen into it by starting to align the texts around selected topics. You can almost predict the "compare and contrast" question on the quiz.

But I am not heading toward a test question. I imitate instead the method of Louis Agassiz by presenting a second fish after arranging for you to stare a while at the first. The second fish is like and unlike its predecessor. There is much to be learned from both similarities and dissimilarities. Of course, my aim is not to help you construct a taxonomy of Christian textual types. I wager instead that a sequence of selected juxtapositions will help you and me appreciate Christian scenes of instruction while exercising us in their reperformance.

I will not play the (Hegelian) game of synthesizing a higher truth out of Gregory and Althaus-Reid. Nor will I try my hand at inclusion and exclusion, deciding who gets to count as a "real Christian" and who not. The same goes for other orthodoxies. Nothing is to be gained by throwing Gregory out on grounds of patriarchy or Platonism. The striking thing about Gregory's remarks against "women" is that he exempts Macrina from them. He cannot square her holiness or her philosophy with what he has been taught about her gender. In the same way, his evident devotion to Plato—his fan's delight in rewriting the details of the *Phaedo*—goes right alongside his conviction that Macrina has gone beyond Socrates. We can skim Gregory's texts looking for reasons not to read him ever again, but it is a wiser use of mortal time to focus on any help he might offer. Does that seem naïve? I'll run the risk. To imagine that we could purify ourselves by purging others is a worse mistake. Communication among humans starts from mixed motives and ends with at least some selfish distortions. To repeat myself: our theology is written and taught under sin. It is, after all, *our* theology.

I do not propose a choice between Gregory and Althaus-Reid. I keep their vivid scenes of bodily instruction side by side. Juxtaposition is the weft of Christian tradition. It is also our cultural condition. We are raised on collage, montage, the quick cut, the sound sample, the teaser-trailer. Just by itself, this quick list of forms should remind us that juxtaposition is not jumble. Unexpected patterns emerge. So do alternatives for our assumptions. For example, both of the texts before us push us to think better about the body in teaching.

Bodily Discipline

Perhaps you remember one violent image from *A Clockwork Orange* (whether novel or film): a prisoner undergoing experimental rehabilitation is strapped to a chair and forced to watch violent films, his eyelids held open by clamps. The image can spring up when I face an audience in a large lecture hall. I am the screen they are compelled to watch.

The typical humanities classroom wants to immobilize students while prying open their eyes and pulling their ears. Is it any wonder that they use a knapsack of electronic devices to escape— or that we now insist on shutting off those too? (A local college advises new teachers to carry a large cardboard box to class. It is to be used for impounding cell phones during the period.) Of all modern classrooms, those dedicated to the humanities may require the most docile bodies—unless we share that distinction with accounting.

Michel Foucault writes acerbically about classroom discipline. He connects it to the training of soldiers, factory workers, and prisoners. For him, micro-regulation of bodies characterizes our sort of late-modern society. Foucault is also fond of pointing out the resemblances between this modern discipline and Christian innovations in controlling bodies. I take Foucault's point but wonder whether he carries it far enough. What strikes me even in current Christian schooling is the unstable combination of different bodily controls.

Consider some of the spaces that make up the "classic" (that is, the 1950s) US seminary: chapel, dining hall or refectory, bedroom, classroom. Each develops specialized bodily controls. The chapel requires a decent order of bodies in worship and private prayer. The dining hall means watchfulness against gluttony (an old sin) and unsociability (a newer one). In the bedroom, the student must guard against the temptations of sex and laziness. It's obvious that different rules have targeted different vices or bodily failings. The table of obstacles or offenses changes with the times. "Laziness" has meant both monastic *acedia* and Calvinist inefficiency. Shouldn't it be just as obvious that sets of seminary rules project their own expectations about how bodies figure in teaching, in learning? And that both teachers and students carry these expectations with them? Imagine yourself in a familiar classroom. Do you *expect* the body seated before you to challenge your teaching most by its ignorance, its lusts, its immersion in matter, its emotional needs, its mortal despair? And what uses is your own body supposed to have for teaching? Christian theologians often say God took flesh to teach flesh. That is a claim about divine love, but also about the capacities of embodiment. A body is a way of learning—and so of teaching.

When we indulge fantasies of the seminaries we are trying to save, which regime of bodies do we imagine to be in control of the classroom? Is it one or another of the older Christian regimes that urged attention, respect, prayerful contemplation?

Or is it a more modern discipline? Stop. Can we any longer distinguish between Christian and university pedagogies? When theology becomes part of the modern university, the conduct of theological classrooms passes under its control. Yet university pedagogy is not evidently a Christian pedagogy—especially in conceiving bodies.

Christian Asceticism

Whatever happens in a classroom is framed by events in the rooms around it. A student who studies systematics in Classroom 101 is also praying in chapel, eating in the community dining hall, studying alongside others in the library, and sleeping in a row of rooms alongside others—separated perhaps by the thinnest of partitions. The classroom study of theology is juxtaposed with other activities, all of which can be called "theology" in a broader sense. On many accounts, this juxtaposition is required for theological erudition to have its full meaning.

In most epochs and places, study of divinity also had a place in time. Advanced study in Christian theology presumed a Christian upbringing—or, at least, pretended that there had been one. There were adult conversions (especially in missionary territories) or late returns to religious practice. Still, embarking on theology presupposed the support of one's community and a history within it. Gregory of Nyssa lays this out (proudly, poignantly) when he retells Macrina's childhood. Her ability to teach him or to lead her community rested on a long apprenticeship.

Such childhoods are now rarer in the United States. Seminaries and divinity schools admit students who lack churched upbringings or adult experience in ordinary congregations. Many students are recent converts—or seekers after conversion. They are passionate but barely instructed and poorly habituated. Those who were raised in Christian communities often show similar gaps. I don't gainsay the religious experiences of my students. (I was an adolescent convert myself and wanted to test a priestly vocation at once.) Still, I notice that the exclusions of university-like classrooms are now reinforced by the absence of Christian apprenticeship.

When I carry a text by Gregory of Nyssa into a classroom, I must somehow reconstitute around it the missing rooms of a community like Macrina's—or the missing years of her upbringing. Often, I can only name their absence. My lectures offer reminders of what it would take to read the text whole—with mind and body both readied by practice. At the same time, I do not want the encounter with Gregory to degenerate into nostalgia. The study of Christian tradition is not collecting curiosities for display cases. I teach Gregory to reactivate his scenes. Scenes of Christian instruction must escape the control of their authors—perhaps especially at points of sharpest authorial anxiety. What is more important, they must expect to be rewritten by a divine teacher, who is and is not bodily.

Bodily Paradoxes

To our eyes, the strongest contrast between the two texts I juxtapose may have to do with decency. Gregory of Nyssa depicts Macrina as a virgin martyr, whose long asceticism was the expression and condition of her wisdom. For Althaus-Reid, the future of theology requires a deliberate indecency, a theology of lust, "per-version," obscenity (each redefined). What could be more obviously opposed?

Let the opposition stand. I see in it at least two points of agreement. The first is the conviction that teaching theology must engage the body. Macrina's body attracts unwanted desires, develops cancers, carries scars, and dies while desiring marriage. Marcella's bodies smell in summer heat, need costumes, have orgasms in unexpected places—and with unapproved partners. All of that must be engaged by any teaching that wants to call itself Christian theology.

The second point of agreement between the two texts is that bodies are not reducible to some simple lesson—perhaps especially not the lessons we think we know about sex. The living body of the learner is not the guild-certified topic of "body theology." (A friend remarks that much seminary talk about "the body" betrays the naïveté of youthful health and frequent bathing. I would add, the invulnerable fantasies of advertising and other "social media.") The actual bodies described or addressed by Christian theology are not tidy. The body of Jesus is familiar, radiant, tortured, unrecognizable. Sometimes he is startled when touched. Sometimes he spits into the soil to make healing paste. He lounges at table with the "unclean." He consorts with the sick. He has, in the canonical Gospels, no sexual relations or desires. According to one old tradition, he was ugly. On other testimony, he carried the wounds of crucifixion even after rising from the dead. That sort of body is theology's assigned object and subject.

Teaching the theology of an incarnate god, we subvert the assumptions about bodily discipline built into contemporary university classrooms. Whether this violates the pact that brought theology into modern universities, I leave for its partisans to litigate. In my experience, the ideal of *Wissenschaft* excludes many older teachings, not just Christian theology. I punch through walls of the standard humanities classroom whether I am teaching Christian Scriptures, Nietzsche, utopian fiction, or the ethics of sex. Still, the exclusion of the body from approved classrooms especially disables Christian pedagogy.

I write those words and immediately acknowledge my own nervousness with unscripted movements in class. I do not like team-spirit "trainings" that rely on compelled exercises. (Falling backward, eyes closed, into what I hope are the waiting hands of my colleagues? You've got to be kidding.) With many other teachers, I fear "losing control" over a classroom—as if I ever could control its most important processes. I further admit that for all the publicity around pedagogical innovation, surveillance over teaching bodies has worsened during my years of university employment. We are filmed for evaluation and then urged to adopt standard voices, expressions, and gestures. Our lectures are supposed to be as entertaining (and formulaic) as TED talks, our visual aids as slick as Super Bowl spots. Students often participate in this disciplining of the teaching body, not least because they have been raised in finicky consumerism. Of course, standardizing surveillance of teaching bodies follows on viewing the teacher as an interchangeable expert or fluent purveyor of required information. Such a teacher has no calling, only functions. Her distinctive gifts, whatever they might have been, are overwritten by mandated training.

At other moments, teaching breaks through in a way that surprises everyone. A few years ago, in a full lecture hall, a student asked me to apply a lesson in the text before us to AIDS activism in the United States during the 1980s. My throat tightened. Tears began to flow. I was overcome by grief. I was also mortified. Finally, I managed to say, "It is hard to talk about that." I stammered a few sentences more about hoping when there was no hope in sight. Fortunately, we were at the end of the class period. The student who posed the question came up immediately to apologize. She added, "But I think I begin to understand what happened." Five years later, another student recalled the moment as the most vivid teaching in the many hours we were together.

Gregory would reprove my tears as he reproved his own. (Marcella and I have cried together over lost friends.) For the moment, I am less interested in defending tears than in remembering my embarrassed surprise at them. I obviously didn't expect the question or prepare a well-formed answer. I am disgusted by even the hint of using *that* grief to "communicate" plotted lessons. At the same time, I recognize the awkward moment as some sort of gift—to the students who noticed it, to myself. Christian education relies on bodies teaching other bodies about an incarnation. There are bound to be a few surprises. Early one morning, for example, a cemetery gardener might be revealed as your hometown rabbi brought back from the dead. Your tears of grief might catch divine light.

Exercise: If there were no university classrooms left for Christian theology, where would you choose to teach it? In a café, a factory, the street, a hospital, a prison, a worship hall, a garden? Would you feel entitled to a salary? How would you regard other Christian teachers? Would you count yourself a member of a profession? What title would you claim beyond the gospel honorific "teacher"? Perhaps "student of the students of God"—without any irony?

Exercise: Try writing theology in the nude. No, really, try it. Even if you have to do it under the covers at bedtime or in a locked bathroom while pretending to shower. Note carefully the range of affects. Are you ashamed? Tongue-tied? Anxious about letting God see you unclothed? Then consider what it would take to begin "dis-covering" your body. Can you see it as something *other than* an object of management, a source of anxiety, a failed commodity, an erotic toy? How many hundreds of hours will you have to write theology in the nude before you really begin?

Exercise: Tell some stories about how words written in the nude might be taught, fully clothed, to a classroom of students who have a reasonable expectation that you will not inflict inappropriate intimacy on them. Does that writing prompt already seem dangerously indecent? Remember Marcella's refrain: Christian theology may require both obscenity and indecency—though not in the ways you expect.

2

Sciences

6

Bonaventure,
The Mind's Path into God

Two years before his "transit" or crossing-over through death, Francis of Assisi was given land on Mount Alverna (its Latin name) for use as a hermitage. His followers later compared the ridge to Mount Sinai, where Moses received the Law, and Mount Tabor, where Jesus was transfigured. A follower of Francis, Bonaventure compiled the Franciscans' official biography of their saintly founder. Here is part of what he tells about events on the latter-day mountain.

Francis and his companion decide to open the Gospels at random in search of divine guidance.[1] Three times the Scriptures offer up descriptions of Christ's last day. After imitating Christ's actions throughout his life, Francis realizes that he must now "be conformed to the afflictions and pains of [Christ's] passion." Sometime later, near mid-September's feast of the holy cross, Francis watches as a bright, burning figure descends from the heavens. When the six-winged seraph draws near, Francis discovers in its wings the representation (*effigies*) of a crucified man. The man looks straight at him. Francis rejoices before compassion pierces him. He is deeply perplexed. How can crucified flesh appear within a seraph's immortal spirit? In that moment, God shows Francis that his friendship with Christ will be sealed, not by physical martyrdom (which Francis has long desired) but by "a burning of his mind that transforms it wholly into the image

59

of Christ crucified." The vision of the seraph disappears, leaving Francis's heart on fire and the physical marks of crucifixion in his hands, feet, and side. The divine "writing" declares love.

Bonaventure is only a child when that teaching event occurs on Francis's mountain. Over the decades following, he becomes a celebrated teacher of theology at an eminent university and then—under obedience—head of the Franciscans. Around the thirty-third celebration of the founder's death, Bonaventure returns to the site of the vision. Worn down, he seeks peace. Meditating on "mental ascents" to God, Bonaventure abruptly understands that Francis's vision is a scene inviting others to enter (prologue no. 2).[2] The seraph's six wings are "steps or routes" by which the soul can "cross over" to peace "through the ecstatic excesses of Christian wisdom" (prol. 3).

Maps and Mirrors

I have moved from Francis's official biography to a short book that Bonaventure wrote about his return to Mount Alverna. The little book's main title is *Itinerarium mentis in Deum*, the *itinerarium* of the mind (in)to God. I risk translating *mens* as "mind" because Bonaventure chooses it over a word for soul. The adjacent word in the title, *itinerarium*, is trickier. It can mean route or way, especially for walking—and Franciscans typically traveled by foot (as Jesus did). Bonaventure associates the root word *iter* with step, as in stepping up. *Itinerarium* can also mean the map of a route. (Bonaventure was familiar with maps adorned by small illustrations of important landmarks.) Finally, most interestingly, *itinerarium* is the word for marching orders or the signal to start a march. Bonaventure's *Itinerarium* is at once route, picture map, and signal.

The book has a second title: *Speculatio pauperis in deserto*, the *speculatio* of the poor man in the wilderness. Usually *speculatio* is rendered as "speculation" or "contemplation," depending on whether the translator wishes to emphasize active reasoning or attentive gazing. *Speculatio* can also be "observation": a *turris speculationis* is an observation tower. In some of its uses, *speculatio* even becomes a synonym for *spectaculum*, "spectacle." These meanings are held together etymologically: *speculatio* is an abstract noun related to the concrete noun for mirror, *speculum*. A more poetic translation of *speculatio*—Bonaventure is nothing if not a poet—might be "mirroring": the mirroring of the poor man in the wilderness—the mirroring he did, the mirroring a reader can still do.

Mirrors multiply. In one sense, the poor man in the wilderness is Francis of Assisi and the *speculatio* is his vision atop Alverna. In another, Bonaventure is a man in need who discovers that Francis's vision is a mirror that anyone can use to seek God's consolation. Again, we are all poor seekers in a wilderness far from the God we so confusedly desire. Jesus of Nazareth joins us: he is the beloved Son "thrown" into the "desert" by the Spirit (Mark 1:12, Vulgate *expellit eum in desertum*). Francis is mirrored in Bonaventure, who addresses humankind as mirrored by the pauper Lord. Each mirror instructs. Together they frame Bonaventure's multiplied scene—or, at least, its first rooms.

Bonaventure reads Francis's story as the picture of an ascent open to all. At the same time, and from the beginning, he insists that the only means of ascent is ardent love of the Crucified. The reader must never fall into the foolishness of believing that it is enough to have "reading without anointing, speculation without devotion, investigation without astonishment, circumspection without exultation, industry without piety, knowledge without love, intelligence without humility, study without divine grace, a mirror (*speculum*) without wisdom divinely inspired" (prol. 4). The string of paired terms, in which the second both qualifies and negates the first, is a prescription for how to read this text usefully.

The scene of instruction set by Bonaventure's *Itinerarium* gathers up ways of imitating Francis. Bonaventure goes in his body to the place where Francis's body was made to resemble the body of Jesus. Bonaventure even speaks a little as Francis did, tethering celestial descriptions to the earth of the Scriptures.

The patterns of imitation are then crossed by urgent limitations or negations, reminders that Francis cannot be followed to the end without self-emptying. If the saint's long imitation of Jesus required at last that he pass through the cross, anyone who follows Francis up the mountain will encounter the divine in wounding intensity.

I dwell on the double title and the example of Francis because they set a rhythm that runs through Bonaventure's measured book. God rests after the six days of creation by blessing a seventh for seeing the stages of goodness together. The rhythm of divine creation-and-rest informs many other sequences, including the main events of salvation history. Within the *Itinerarium*, it becomes the pattern and even the means for human learning.

To call learning a "journey" by steps is, for Bonaventure, no trite analogy. Following the map, the learner's mind becomes a mirror. It reflects the route along which she travels. Her contemplation narrates and then recapitulates. It also discloses the first principles on which compelling teaching must depend. A *scientia* or body of teachable knowledge is an ordered series of demonstrations that leads from principles to conclusions. (Demonstration is particularly elegant teaching.) To know a science is to grasp its principles in a way that allows you to lay out their implications or sequels. You ascend to principles and descend to deductions or applications. The alternation of motion and rest, of map and mirror, is the basic rhythm of learning and teaching.

Moving Hierarchies

If you and I were going through the *Itinerarium* together, we would be up at the blackboard redrawing hierarchies or else handing graph paper back and forth. It may be just as well that we cannot do that on this page, since any reader of Bonaventure risks becoming lost in obsession with details. (The risk is greatly multiplied for those of scholarly disposition.) Still, reading his text requires working through some part of it carefully enough to see two things: the details signify, and they signify more as the reader learns more. Bonaventure's cascading lists are mobile arguments about how to activate different bodies of knowledge in pursuit of Christ. Each of them expands as you pay more attention to it. They move even as you read: Bonaventure runs the hierarchies early on, then walks up them again, slowly, as the chapters follow one another.

The opening sections of the book's first chapter preview the comprehensive hierarchies for the mind's ascent. By "hierarchy" I don't mean a structure of power or authority, like a church bureaucracy. The word's original sense comes from theology: a holy ordering. It is holy not least because it pulls toward divinity. The steps, stages, or ladders in Bonaventure never suggest that the power to climb them resides in the reader. Ascent is the hierarchy's own power. Bonaventure underlines this when he fits these patterns to the wings of the seraph. Wings move, pulling and pushing to fly. So, too, the created world's structures lift readers toward the Creator.

The "ladder of the wholeness of all things" matches states of the human soul (1.2): the soul was made to read the created order as one long exhortation to join God in blessed rest. The deep direction at the core of things is recapitulated in Christ's incarnation, which is not for Bonaventure so much a response to contingent sin as a consummating declaration of divine love. Incarnation is as much a part of the original divine plan as creating human beings able to relate to the world by body, spirit, and mind. Bonaventure aligns the main bodies of knowledge recognized by his contemporaries with the soul's powers. He ends the first chapter with theology's manners of teaching and the stages of spiritual transformation. In a few lines, then, he has previewed the book's parallel scenes. He has also provoked the erudite: Francis's vision accommodates everything they teach in universities.

To this point, I have described only Bonaventure's prologue and the introductory sections of one chapter—neither of them exhaustively. Any detailed commentary would be much longer than the *Itinerarium* itself. Bonaventure writes with a dynamic compression that is intended to keep the reader moving. To explain what he abbreviates, to slow the pace for annotation, releases the coiled learning. Implied details spring out like a jack-in-the-box that cannot be put back.

Bonaventure's meditations in chapters 1–6 lead the reader through the principal headings of a complete pattern of human knowledge. The *Itinerarium* is a difficult text for modern readers not so much because it is "religious" or "prayerful" as because it directs prayer through a unified arrangement of bodies of knowledge. Few contemporary Christians believe that prayer can engage the details of natural sciences. Fewer still believe that such sciences cohere with each other or the moth-eaten humanities.

How did Bonaventure's early readers respond to this deft assembly of all received learning into an ascent? It is hard to say. We can be sure that the effect is different for those of us who know mere scraps of medieval learning—and then as historical scholarship rather than as elements of cosmic truth. More: Bonaventure's project has been undone by changes in the very idea of intellectual structure. Would it be possible to rewrite an *Itinerarium* for today? We have no strong sense of unity among bodies of learning, and often feel no ascending purpose in them.

If we cannot read the *Itinerarium* adeptly or rewrite it convincingly, we might still consider by analogy the sort of effect that Bonaventure hoped to produce in his best-schooled readers. Did he want readers to summon their previous studies in order to discover a pattern they had overlooked? He might be saying, "You have missed the figure in the details. You have failed to appreciate the whole." Or is his review of the main sciences a form of consolation? "There is nothing to fear. Christ is there underneath all the rest." Both readings fit the text. So does another. The *Itinerarium* often resembles exercises repeated with graded difficulty—lengthening sprints or jumps over stepped hurdles. Bonaventure says, "Take whatever you know—it doesn't matter what—and follow its larger sequences. You will find yourself lifted up toward the mind's source."

The source of intelligibility, on Bonaventure's account, is the Creator of human souls matched to their world. Everything the Creator makes is in Their image, though not in the same way. Every aspect of the world can be a teaching scene. The soul's ascent ends in a paradox: the face of the Crucified interrupting and yet fulfilling the burning brightness of the seraph.

Dark Light

Bonaventure's seventh chapter is a Sabbath. Having traced the ranks of creation as a divine curriculum, the reader comes to rest. Only this Sabbath must follow a Good Friday, the day of Christ's execution. The reader can reach it only by going beyond familiar science. The final room of Bonaventure's scenes of instruction is union with Christ on the cross.

Here Bonaventure's writing becomes achingly liturgical. The temptation is to quote him—though his lines resist translation in the way that poetry does. I reproduce as I can his advice to those who enter upon the final scene (7.6):

> If you ask how these things are done, question
> Grace, not teaching
> Desire, not understanding
> The groan of prayer, not the study of reason
> The spouse, not the teacher
> God, not man
> Smoke-dark, not brightness
> Not light, but the fire that completely inflames and
>   carries to God by exceeding anointings and
>   burning affections.

The line spacing is mine, not Bonaventure's. I use modern poetic forms to convey the rhythm that builds through the short, contrasting phrases only to break out—break down—in the final reversal: "not light, but the fire . . ." The six previous "nots" have introduced the second clause of each pair. For the seventh—Sabbath—the "not" moves to the front. It responds to the seeking implied in the verb, "question." Questioning is even more the basis of Bonaventure's teaching than of ours, since "the question" (*quaestio*) was the basic unit for both his university classrooms and learned writing. This *quaestio* ends with fire that does not cast light. It burns itself into minds and, sometimes, into hands or feet. The fire: it is at once the burning bush that speaks to Moses, the pillar that leads the Israelites after Egypt, God on Sinai, the altar fires that scorch Levitical sacrifices, the chariot that Ezekiel sees in vision, the refiner's fire in Malachi.

What then is the point of the first six chapters? Why perform the masterful gathering of arts and sciences if the teaching must end beyond them? They set the rhythm of seeing that carries a reader beyond sight. Poetic beats intensify in the little book's last lines because they help the soul move into a darkness where there are no pictures, where the map stops at the edge of the page. The reader must be *carried* across Christ's death by affection expressed and urged on in an intensifying beat.

Perhaps I can say that more academically—which is not necessarily to say it more accurately. Bonaventure reinterprets the paradox of instruction under grace as a paradox of science confronted with a singular, suffering body. Bonaventure's hierarchies reconcile human knowledge to Christ by showing how learning leads back not only to a creator but to a redeemer. Follow any line of truth and you will end up on Golgotha. You can profess all human knowledge, but you must still enter the refiner's fire. The Great Scene of instruction is not a universal encyclopedia but a frightening redemption enacted long ago—and each today—outside Jerusalem.

If it is not possible to rewrite the whole of the *Itinerarium* in our present, it might still be possible to translate that ending. It should not be segregated—or dismissed—as a "mystical experience," whatever people think they mean by that phrase. The end of the *Itinerarium* calls all minds to follow Jesus in discipleship. Discipleship is a fancy way of describing what it is to remain always a student. You can get on the road to Jerusalem wherever you begin to learn, because genuine learning puts you in touch with truth. The farther you advance, the more you realize that all the truths—all roads—lead to the same destination. The times and places of teaching coalesce. Mount Sinai is Mount Tabor and also Golgotha. An early legend says that Adam was buried just where the cross would be pounded into the dry dirt for Jesus of Nazareth. The dark fire of that embodied teaching—easy to lose among imperial atrocities—gives life to your bones.

Paul Tillich,
The Courage to Be

Picking up a book that I once embraced but haven't touched in years, I hesitate to open it. I worry that it will no longer cast its spell. Perhaps I'll be embarrassed by my passionate attachment to something that now draws me not at all.

Take Hermann Hesse. As an undergraduate I raced through his books, beginning with *Steppenwolf*. (In those days, you couldn't enter a student diner without meeting an ostentatiously tattered copy of the novel on a nearby table. Coffee rings on the cover were stripes for service.) I went on to *Demian*, *Siddhartha*, *Narcissus and Goldmund*, even *Beneath the Wheel*—Hesse's melodrama about a seminary student crushed by overwork. Of it, I retain only the scene of an oral examination: the protagonist turns back as he leaves the committee room because he has just recalled a forgotten conjugation in Greek. (In my college dreams, I would sometimes attempt the maneuver but always garbled the conjugation.) Hesse's *Glass Bead Game* draws me back every few years by its consoling imagination of intellectual life. As for his other novels—I hesitate to open them.

A similar hesitation stops me before books of academic theology widely praised one or two generations before mine. Consider Paul Tillich's book *The Courage to Be*.[1] The latest edition offers testimonies to the book's power. They come from theologians I respect. For example, Harvey Cox writes movingly about Tillich's teaching presence through the text. He insists that the book drew him to study with the man.[2] Still, when I pick up *The Courage to Be*, I am put off. Something about its language is too neat—like voice-overs in 1950s' "educational" films. In short, I cannot imagine Tillich's book changing lives. But it did. So, I reperform its teaching in hopes of discovering what I have missed.

The Courage to Be began as a series of teaching scenes in an obvious sense. Its first version consisted of scripts for lectures that Tillich gave at Yale in 1950. The Terry Lectures were supposed to aid "the building of the truths of science and philosophy into the structure of a broadened and purified religion."[3] Tillich immediately recast the lecture scripts as a book, first published in 1952. I underline the dates because the texts address current (Euro-American) conditions: the cultural "death of God," a resulting anxiety, and the rise of armed collectivism that had recently incinerated cities and erected networks of death camps.

Tillich faced memories of recent war with the authority of his own experience. He taught in America as one of many exiles from Nazi Germany. Shortly after Hitler became chancellor of Germany, Tillich was fired from his university post at Frankfurt for vocal criticism of the Nazi Party. Reinhold Niebuhr took him the offer of a position at Union Theological Seminary in New York. (During the Great Depression, the Union faculty voted itself a 5 percent pay *cut* to fund Tillich's salary. That act is its own scene of instruction.) Tillich was then forty-seven. Moving to Union meant mastering both a new language and a new intellectual context. In 1959, his success was certified by the cover of *Time* magazine.[4]

The yellow band on the cover proclaims "A Theology for PROTESTANTS." The caption suggests a scene of instruction at a national scale and across many denominations (though not all). We can pine for a time when Christian teaching was counted so broadly persuasive, but I hope to separate the machinery of publicity from Tillich's own teaching scenes. Even with an author so famous and widely remembered (if not always fondly), I want to picture instruction in the books.

The Convergence of Fields

To begin, Tillich quotes another part of the writing cue for the Terry series. He is to address "religion in the light of science and philosophy" (3). He adds immediately: "I have chosen a concept in which theological, sociological and philosophical problems converge, the concept of 'courage.' Few concepts are as useful for the analysis of the human situation." Tillich will focus on the point at which three important bodies of knowledge converge. Convergence is not conceptual fusion. In chapter 3, for example, Tillich takes pains to separate pathological anxiety, treated by physicians and therapists, from existential anxiety, studied by theologians and ministers. At other times, and notably in chapter 5, Tillich moves discoveries from one field into another—or at least puts two fields into conversation. For example, he is eager that Christian theologians should engage with "existentialist" art and literature—then current versions of the modern.

Tillich's procedure for sorting concepts across disciplines contrasts sharply with Bonaventure's recapitulation of the hierarchy of sciences. Tillich does not want to show that sociology, philosophy, or even academic theology points toward some higher end. Each discipline appears instead as a distinct sphere. Tillich traces variations in concepts—or at least terms—across spheres. His path is more horizontal than vertical. The spheres are not ladders or hierarchies or paired wings. They are "fields": adjacent plots of land separately cultivated. Tillich moves across them as a surveyor who has the advantage of a wider view and a talent for climbing fences.

Tillich's survey leaves his own book off the map. In Bonaventure, the language of the *Itinerarium* is secured by its dependence on both Scripture and theology. What language does Tillich use to write about the convergence of problems from different fields? His book recognizes a crisis of meaning, but then it floats just above, offering broad judgments on philosophical movements or the significance of European and American histories.

To my ears, the voice is distinctly professorial, if closer to the public lecture than the specialist monograph. I count off tics of academic style: frequent pauses for explicit definition; taxonomies used for classifying thinkers (chiefly with "-ism" terms); personification of historical periods ("the whole period believed"); and so on. I wonder whether the very familiarity of these tics is meant to soothe the audience or the reader. The authorial voice explains gravely what has happened to culture but then beckons toward a recognizable future. It is like someone standing up in the rubble left by a catastrophe to say, "Here's what we have to do. You three go find water and tinned foods. You over there, see if you can start the generator. Does anyone know how to bandage wounds? Who will comfort the children?" Tillich's voice is like that, sounding confidently over the debris of recent war and mounting uncertainty. Imagine him saying: "This is where our cultural history has stranded us. Though it looks as if our shared projects have shattered, we can still go forward—as we can prevent the catastrophe from happening again." In such a moment, even pedantry can console.

I don't mean to *dismiss* Tillich as a pedant. If I were judging that figure, I would choose a more exaggerated caricature. University life supplies many. (A good satire of academic voices might have to solve some psychological puzzles. Why, for example, is a blend of tedious obsession and irritable dogmatism the regular voice on so many lecture stages? And why do some students find that performance alluring enough to copy for another lifetime?) If Tillich adopts some devices of academic rhetoric, he avoids many others. Still, it interests me that he chooses standard pedagogical gestures when composing an exhortation to existential courage. He wants to commend courage by expounding its *concept*.

Teachers carry both the habits of their training and the fantasies that drew them to it. More than most, Tillich scrutinizes his own habits of mind—his capacities and attractions, temptations and routine failures. He also attributes central insights to experiences with the "creative arts." His notion of revelation as breakthrough, for example, comes from seeing "how the substance of a work of art could destroy form" in "creative ecstasy."[5] Why then does Tillich restrain himself from destroying theology's standard forms? Perhaps it is his confidence that some *synthesis* could encompass even the abyss or that there could be a *system* of existential truth. Or perhaps Tillich held the sacrificial hope that dying pedagogical roles could open a path through charred institutions as a final gift or act of repentance.

What scene of instruction does Tillich's exhorting voice project in *Courage*? Its calm is abstract, universal. Tillich draws no attention to himself—to his exiled body standing before an American audience (restless or still) in a particular room (drafty or overheated) on the Yale campus. The space projected around the voice is featureless and unbounded. (In a television studio, it is called an "infinity" background. Not the intensive infinity of the living God but a surfaceless color receding without seams.) Tillich speaks from and to an undifferentiated "we." He leads "us" to recognize deep causes in a cultural situation that is presumed to affect evenly all who hear or read.

Contrast this projected scene with the biographical specificity that opens the *Itinerarium*. Bonaventure, weighed down by care, retreats to the mountain where Francis received a vision. Bonaventure yearns after peace. He loves Francis. They both love Christ, whose face is inscribed in the seraph's paradoxical beauty. Christ is the way into the Trinity that lures all creation. Links of desire motivate ascent along the hierarchies that Bonaventure traces upward on every side of the reader. Tillich begins with no such story of lived desire. He has been assigned a topic. In response, he has chosen to talk about a "concept"—courage—because it will be useful in analyzing the human situation. What desire does the preface disclose or call forth? What does a conceptual analysis of the human situation promise to the individual hearer or reader?

You may be wondering whether I will fault Tillich next for adopting certain Enlightenment notions about the universality of reason before pointing out how culturally bounded they actually are. My worry—or my puzzlement—looks in another direction. I am struck by how *disincarnate* Tillich's scene of instruction has become. How are bodies arranged within it? How are they characterized—unless perhaps as point-selves on a segment of cultural history labeled "Age of Anxiety"? How does he expect to motivate his embodied hearers or readers—unless his main offer is just to reduce their anxiety? What impulse will move them through his words toward courage—or God? I am struck again by the difference in rhythm between Bonaventure's text and Tillich's. If a beat can keep a body walking into darkness, how is one moved by conceptual history? Is a clarified history supposed to carry us—forward?

Familiar Structure, New Language

The structure of Bonaventure's *Itinerarium* may be its most dazzling accomplishment. That cannot be said of *The Courage to Be*. Tillich's structure leads by accustomed steps, not dramatic leaps or splendid disclosures—much less by ecstasies. If he frequently professes his attachment to existentialist literature, he does not imitate its forms.

The Courage to Be is divided by topic into six chapters—by topic, but also sometimes chronologically, since many chapters are historical surveys. Both topical division and historical survey are standard patterns for current academic books. Tillich's chapters are further arranged into two sets of three each. The first set is definitional: it clarifies concepts and stipulates meanings. It also presents the reader with the book's main characters: two concepts, courage and anxiety. The concept of courage is expanded by recalling its history. (No detailed history is provided for the concept of anxiety.) The reader is taught to recognize "existential" meanings as opposed to superficial ones. Why does that matter? More than an ethical virtue, existential courage is an ontological stance, a way of being. It is not chiefly self-control with regard to fear; it is self-affirmation in the face of anxiety. By taking on anxiety, a person prepares for more creative being.

The book's second set of chapters explains how to begin to

practice such courage. Chapter 4 wants to show that the courage to be *as a part*, carried to radical extremes, becomes either totalitarian collectivism or American conformism. Chapter 5 argues that extreme versions of the courage to be *as oneself* transfer divine self-grounding to the human being, which cannot sustain it. These two chapters are historical arguments about what becomes of important nineteenth-century forms of courage: revolutionary courage becomes Stalinism and Nietzschean courage—so Tillich claims—becomes Nazism. Chapter 6 shows the way forward. What "we" need now is a courage able to transcend both extremes—the courage *to accept acceptance*, which is an absolute faith. The argument of the last three chapters has something like this form: "I will describe your impasse to you. You might conclude that advancing means going this way or that. Both are dead ends. The only way out is to pass through your doubt along a third way. For that you will need courage."

The means of persuasion in these chapters are modest. Sometimes Tillich will issue an invitation through a description. Consider the opposition of death and creation in these two sentences: "The ground of everything that is[,] is not a dead identity without movement and becoming; it is living creativity. Creatively it affirms itself, eternally conquering its own nonbeing" (33). A life of ongoing creation is something that the reader is supposed to want. So are active freedom and release from anxiety. Tillich further supposes that the reader has already chosen to join those who face up to the present rather than fleeing from it. In an age of anxiety, the reader wants (or should want) to belong to those "of us [who] do look" directly at its causes (58). Most of all, Tillich's ideal reader seeks (or should seek) a future that avoids the horrors of the wartime just past. The reader is invited into the historical moment that struggles to survive cataclysm. Bonaventure's ascents culminate in an exhortation to enter the narrative of Christ's passion. For Tillich, a more powerful narrative is human history, which must be understood and then acted upon.

As it nears the end of *The Courage to Be*, Tillich's voice outstrips soothing analysis. If he indulges the pedantry of definition,

Tillich recasts key words. His justification for doing so becomes a refrain: since central Christian terms have "lost their genuine meaning," Christians need new words (47). Sometimes Tillich speaks Christianity in the language of French existentialism. On other pages he tries for a go-between language that will stitch together theology, philosophy, sociology, psychotherapy, and existentialist literature. He does not hesitate to reach for lessons in poems, novels, or plays. "Modern art is not propaganda but revelation. . . . It shows that the reality of our existence is as it is" (136). If this suggests some likeness between modern art and Tillich's writing, the likeness is conceptual, not formal—is bare truth, not an icing of beauty.

By the time a reader reaches the end of *The Courage to Be*, with its critique of the God of traditional theism, she realizes how consequential Tillich's new language for truth can be. The definition that most needs changing is for the word "divine." As Tillich speaks, God becomes the ground of being, a living creativity conquering its own nonbeing. The creative *human* self is not defined by gifts of grace and redemption; it is said to be "centered." Religion is redescribed as "the state of being grasped by the power of being-itself" (144). Tillich applies formal invention not to structure, narrative, or image but to accurate terminology. His enemy is not ugliness but cliché, whether sentimental or authoritarian.

A new language displaces an old one. What looks in Tillich like academic blandness might be in fact linguistic iconoclasm. The featureless lecture hall that Tillich's professorial voice projects is like a Gothic cathedral stripped of its "idols" by zealous Reformers. What scene of instruction do they leave behind? Once the iconoclasts have come and gone—when a scared few gather again in a warehouse of plaster shards, splintered wood, jumbled glass-chips—how does Christian teaching start up again? What desire remains after severe purification?

The ruins in which Tillich stands to lecture were made by historical cataclysm. He rises to teach in the twilight of Christian idols—impotent artifacts of older theology. What words can he use, unless perhaps words begged from other fields?

Tillich's End

Not all in Tillich is remaking. In the last chapter, as he takes long strides toward new formulations, he retrieves Luther as an emblem of the contemporary situation. The German Reformer becomes the forerunner of modernity, the example of courage and action "in spite of" (148-49, 156-57). Luther will act as a Christian in spite of the fact that he is still a sinner. We too can act with Luther-like courage, Tillich suggests, even though it is no longer possible to trust in the God of any traditional theology. The last sentence of the book—italicized by Tillich—is both famous and enigmatic. It reads, *"The courage to be is rooted in the God who appears when God has disappeared in the anxiety of doubt"* (175).

One way to read the sentence is as a translation of Luther for modern ears: "Here is what Luther's theology of the hidden God sounds like when you speak it into the acoustics of anxiety." Still, I suspect that the Reformer is retrieved into this book as confirmation, not as authorizing principle. While Tillich secures in Luther a convincing example of courage, he does not need Luther to prove the truth of what he has established by historical and cultural analyses.

On another reading, the book's last sentence abandons the main categories of inherited Christian doctrine. You might compare it to Kant explaining the ethical content behind the improbable myths in Christian Scriptures. "Here," Kant sometimes seems to say, "this is what those barbarous (and suspiciously empirical) stories in the Bible are really about." So, too, Tillich might mean: "The death of the theistic God, of the traditional God of Christian theology so far, actually reveals the truths of our situation."

This second reading tries to resolve persistent doubts about Tillich's multiple languages. In *The Courage to Be*, which language is the "text" and which the "translation"? Is traditional Christian language still the original and Tillich's new language a concession to the tinnitus of modern ears? Or does his new language replace the older language of justification by faith alone, the theology of the cross, the hidden God? If strong theological language always responds to specific circumstances, are all strong theological languages *equal* so far as they respond adequately to their times? Or is Tillich's language for us truer than the earlier languages, deformed as they were by unsuspected idolatry and cravings for institutional triumphs?

Some help for these questions might be had from a third reading of the final sentence—and a return to the juxtaposition with Bonaventure. Perhaps Tillich's conclusion pictures a motion through anxiety into something beyond. It would then be tempting to see resemblances between Tillich's disappearing God and the crucified God at the end of the *Itinerarium*. There are differences, of course. In Bonaventure, the ascending mind stretches at last beyond knowledge into a passionate darkness— but it is still *theology* all the way. For Tillich in *The Courage to Be*, the resolution of existential courage abandons the God of theology, along with the particularities of incarnation. (I should remind you that I always talk about particular books. So, here, I am not trying to describe "Tillich's thought" so much as the pedagogical sequence of *The Courage to Be*.) In Tillich's lectures, it is as if theology (or at least academic theology) is abandoned along with its cultured despisers. The concept of courage runs through theology, sociology, philosophy, but the *deed* of courage must be accomplished beyond them. This is not the dark light of Bonaventure's road to Golgotha. It is the courage to reassemble fragments boldly. (*Loque fortiter!*) Tillich's pedagogy assumes that traditional Christianity must be released together with its rival sciences. It must be relinquished because history has broken it beyond present fixing.

8

Theology and
the Limits of Knowing(ness)

Whatever the prevailing or predicted relations of Christian theology to dominant models for higher learning, teachers of theology must contend daily with rival bodies of knowledge—their contents, logics, and pedagogies. If you intend to commend transformative lessons or compose persuasive books, you have to confront the forms of knowledge already imposed on your hearers or readers. The earnest student who decides to reject worldly knowledge in favor of the pure gospel still carries the impress of earlier schooling—not to mention, the current categories of her mother tongue. So does the teacher, who has excelled at other kinds of study before undertaking academic theology—and excelled at an approved theology before being accredited to teach. Deep education is reeducation. A theology that wants to persuade the world must make its place in the middle of what the world counts as learning.

Theological Writing and Cultural Diagnosis

Where do you begin to change theology after the collapse of so many systems of dogma, within post-Christian cultures dominated by technical expertise? According to a familiar narrative, the bodies of knowledge around us have effectively superseded Christian thinking. Christianity can no longer claim to be news for "Western civilization." Most of what it has to say for itself is prelabeled as bigoted ignorance. Of course, this narrative too shows signs of wear. The story of "secularization" (to give it another name) has its own disappointments to explain. Our liberation from priests and kings—or puritans and revivalists—has left many hungrier than they were. In the preface to *Zarathustra*, Nietzsche describes the cultural present as the loss of every ideal beyond the nihilism of the swarm. In the *Glass Bead Game*, Hesse's narrator from the future consigns the present decades to "the age of *feuilleton*"—that is, the online post. In *1984*, Orwell represents not only our political oppressions but our debased. language. Dethroning Theology as "queen of the sciences" has led in our between-times not to the coronation of Reason or Art or even Good Sex, but to brand management.

Perhaps we should revisit not just narratives of secularization but the managerial assumptions in telling grand histories. Stories about God's disappearance from cultures dependent on Europe have already called forth many religious responses, Tillich's among them. The responses have not so far succeeded in stopping the decline of older Christian institutions. Of course, if the historical shifts are indeed so vast, it makes no sense to draft strategic plans for reversing them. A few dazzling books, innovative curricula, or proposals for better funding cannot reverse tectonic shifts. It is also too late to greet the shifts with cries of surprise. The disruption of theological schooling began many decades ago for historically prominent denominations. The institutional endings around us arrive in slow motion.

If we abandon easy cultural diagnoses, if we put aside our rehearsed laments, it may still make sense to ask a smaller question: Can we stage persuasive scenes of theological instruction within the "epistemic shifts," underneath them, alongside them? To ask that question well requires that we press on the constraints carried by the word "can." For example, what relation do we picture between institutions and scenes of instruction? If all existing Christian seminaries and schools of divinity disappeared overnight, what exactly would prevent us from reactivating theological scenes elsewhere? What cultural prejudices about education or the forms of knowledge would we have to overcome to do so? Preoccupation with the fate of existing institutions conceals more urgent questions about how to teach theology's ways of knowing within the growing cynicism about any licensed knowledge.

I want to escape from two ways of telling our situation: "The culture is wicked and so hates Christian truth" and "Christianity has been disproved by science or history." Both of these plots for history are simplistic. They are also tired—or "lame." The plot that Christian teaching must now actually engage begins something like this: "The world has up to now been ruled by systems of oppressive power that we can escape only by joining the people who like what we like—and then waiting on our vindication by events."

I can say this less severely. Teaching in a US classroom in these latter days means confronting economic, ecological, and political anxieties at high pitch. It also demands an ingenuity that can circumvent distraction and cynicism. But most of all, a contemporary teacher must be able to confront boredom with supposedly depleted languages. What we need is not a narrative of "secularization" or even late capitalism. Much less do we need Christian denunciations of cultural depravity or lamentation over the triumph of science. (Other laments are still necessary. I have sampled a few already.) We need a story about how we have forgotten that words sometimes carry the weight of all flesh.

We need the story, and we are the ones to tell it. One advantage we can claim from theology's diminishing status is greater freedom to make a place for it among the contending programs of expertise. If theology is being squeezed out of universities, perhaps that should remind us that it never really fit within them. Bonaventure's *Itinerarium* is constructed around paradoxes: a suffering human face within the seraph's incandescent wings, a path to life that runs through death. At the end of Tillich's *Courage to Be*, God can appear only because God has disappeared. If theology must begin in the middle of current arts and sciences, it always ends beyond them. Teachers of theology cannot expect to find its perfect place in human hierarchies of learning. There is no perfect place inside. The challenge is rather to find useful starting places from which to lead learners outside.

Over centuries, Christian writers have started from analogies to existing bodies of knowledge. They have tried to say what theology looks like—at least, for beginners. One common analogy has likened theology to philosophy, though the implications of the analogy have gyrated with changing definitions of philosophy. But we should remember other analogies. For example, the four "doctors" or teachers of the Latin-speaking churches were each trained principally in rhetoric (Jerome, Ambrose, Augustine, Gregory the Great). Other writers have relied on comparisons with medicine or natural science. At present, in many US schools, authoritative models come from therapy or a mix of social science and political theory. Each of these analogies does some work in introducing theology. Still, I find that (my) theology's look-alike is literature.

I'm not proposing a return to "narrative theology" or "theology as story." The literature I have in mind is often deliberately antinarrative: its stories trace labyrinths. I'm thinking of experimental fiction, fragmented testimony, cinematic montage, artistic assemblage or collage. When I ask students to write a formal paper on a topic in systematic theology, the result is often lifeless. But when I give them just seven minutes of class time to invent a prophetic character for our present, they astonish me and themselves. If (our) academic theology often lacks shape and texture, if it can no longer move us, part of the problem may be that we keep trying to force it into the wrong mold.

Mutations of Knowledge and Knowingness

The distance from Bonaventure to Tillich can be measured in the changed bodies of knowledge around them. There are obvious shifts in *contents*. The physics that Bonaventure recapitulates is not the physics that Tillich accepts. Again, Tillich's "sociology" has no match in Bonaventure's scheme. As contents mutate, whole sciences appear and disappear.

There are also large-scale changes in the *character* of knowledge—say, in the expectations that determine whether something can count as a science. The modified Aristotelian logic that organizes thirteenth-century physics does not envisage the same sort of intelligibility as the mathematical physics of Newton and Laplace or Einstein and Heisenberg.

Finally, perhaps least obviously, bodies of knowledge change in relation to the *forms of power* flowing through them. New forms of power require new forms of science for their aggressive flourishing. The complex interactions of church and monarchy that play above and around Bonaventure dictate one arrangement of knowledge; the imperial coalitions of centralized nation-states that ravage Tillich's world dictate another.

These simple reminders about the historical mutations of knowledge issue in an equally simple point: changes at any level of knowledge reconfigure the space for Christian theology.

What kind of knowledge does a teacher need about how knowledge has changed between the texts being taught and the present classroom? What kind of knowledge *can* she have? Again, what assumptions do we make about our ability to counteract the trending intellectual vices—in our students or in our field? Each of these questions may encourage the facile answers of knowingness, not least in proposals for curricular reform. We can approach them more modestly in reflection—or private conversation. Faculty members often complain to one another about students. Underneath complaint, you hear worry, uncertainty, anxieties over change. No course works the same way when it is repeated. There are different students in it—and there are ongoing cultural mutations around both students and teachers.

Nostalgic fantasy would persuade us that theological projects have become more challenging since the European Middle Ages. We are told that Bonaventure or Thomas Aquinas achieved a "synthesis" of all other knowledge under the beneficent superintendence of Christian theology. Fantasy sighs: if only we could get back there! To which there are two answers: we can't, and that's not how things were. There were innumerable critics in Bonaventure's own university willing to point out all the things he had trimmed or omitted while building his hierarchies. Thomas Aquinas's *Summa theologiae*, often touted as the monument of Scholastic synthesis, is actually a long effort to simplify by careful exclusion. (Even by medieval standards, the remarkable thing about Thomas is not how much natural science he includes, but how much he is able to explain with the little that he quotes.) There has never been a time when Christian theology held the whole of human knowledge in tranquil possession. Its efforts to police other sciences have seldom been received with gratitude.

The *intellectual* history of theology shows a long series of collaborations with social norms and political powers but also with learned guilds and scientific styles. Well before Schleiermacher, theologians had to negotiate some room for themselves in evolving institutions of higher learning. The room has never been uncontested—not now, not then. Many Christian theologians have taught against, outside, or above the available varieties of worldly wisdom. Bonaventure's *Itinerarium* ends in a lyrical sequence of quotations from Scripture, which remains the privileged speech even of excess. His contemporary and counterpart, Thomas Aquinas, begins his *Summa* by constructing an analogy between theology and human sciences. In his account, theology is at once like, unlike, and beyond ordered bodies of human knowledge. For both Bonaventure and Thomas, Christian theology sets the limits of ordinary knowledge, marking boundaries it cannot pass, correcting conclusions that it draws in ignorance of revelation. Beyond the boundary, theological language undoes itself by more thorough unsaying. Even the languages of the Scriptures remain human language. The best theology is ready to relinquish scriptural locutions in hopes of experiencing sharper love.

"The best theology," I say, betraying my own judgments. Much of theology is not the best. It is self-contented orthodoxy or preening erudition or punishing prescription. Because Christian theology remains an all-too-human science, it incurs its own history of power. It censors speech and punishes bodies. Theology taught seriously always risks becoming coercion—that is, tyranny.

Changes in knowledge alter theology's characteristic vices. If arrogance and vanity always afflict it, they favor different costumes. (Pull from the shelves a history of academic regalia or notice the recent trend toward customized doctoral gowns that advertise each institution. I now have the chance to buy a robe that would, with a matching mask, serve for Venetian Carnival. As if burnt orange weren't costume enough.) In my students, in myself, I detect the reigning vices under a very literal *knowingness*—the confidence, fueled by the demand to "comment" instantly on everything, that you know at once what you think, that you have polished opinions always to hand.

In online "discussions" about religious topics, everyone gets to play an inquisitor. I am tempted to rewrite what Adam Phillips says about psychoanalytic knowingness. Theology can be good for showing how certain claims gain authority, but it is *too* good at claiming authority for itself. By combining its languages with unlikely terminologies, by speaking its truths in unexpected places, theology "can be relieved of the knowingness that makes it look silly."[1] After all, if Christian theologians are experts about anything, it must be at knowing that there are no human experts when it comes to being fully human.

On my most sympathetic reading, Tillich speaks repeatedly against knowingness. He insists that a teaching able to address existential anxiety not set itself up as a self-contented academic field alongside the others. Tillich tunes his voice to the needs of an anxious decade after great horrors. He is bold enough to suggest that catastrophe may bring advantages for teaching theology. If it cancels the tacit treaties between churches and other regimes, then it may open space for teaching otherwise. The distance from Bonaventure to Tillich or from Tillich to now might be measured in improved prospects for teaching. There has never been a better time for showing what kind of knowledge theology isn't.

Exercise: Draw a picture of a "hierarchy of knowledge"—either the ranking accepted in the institution that houses you or the pattern of your own learning. Where do you put theology? (Or is theology kept hidden among the arts that you set to the side, as private delights? Like binge watching Hollywood *noir*.) Do you still believe that there is knowledge beautiful enough to lure you through your fears, your despairs? Does it lure you to an "academic" life?

Exercise: List the intellectual vices that most annoy you in your colleagues. Rank them at first from most annoying to least, then from most common to rarest. How many of those vices do you find in yourself? Have they worsened with "experience"?—Bonus question: What common vices have you activated in addressing the previous questions?

3

Moving Pictures

9

Teresa of Ávila,
The Interior Castle

Modern readers often take Augustine's *Confessions* as the story of a conversion. In fact, the book recalls several. It also reflects on the unpredictable effects of conversion stories. Readers get a dramatic narrative about the life change of the great monk, Antony, and then another, equally dramatic, about how Antony's biography turns its readers' lives. When I read the *Confessions*, I am drawn to the story of Alypius, Augustine's faithful, diffident friend. (I sympathize entirely too much with impulsive aesthetes.) If Augustine had to be won over to the sober beauties of sexual restraint, Alypius had to overcome an addiction to spectacle—to enacted "pictures."

Augustine includes Alypius's story in part to caution against the lush excesses of imagination—dangerous in rhetoric but also in poetry. Elsewhere in the *Confessions*, Augustine accuses poetry of authorizing immorality. Depicting Jupiter as an adulterer, it hints that the god's acts might excuse human wickedness. Augustine recalls lines from the poet Terence, in which a "worthless young man" points to a wall painting of Jupiter's seduction of Danaë to justify his own fornications. As part of his rhetorical training, Augustine was once compelled to perform poetry's theater. "It was assigned me . . . that I should speak the words of Juno enraged and grieving that she 'could not keep the Trojan king out of Italy.'" The task was not to recite Virgil but to perform a prose paraphrase of the opening scene of the *Aeneid*. "And he was said to be more praiseworthy who with the dignity of the depicted character excelled in likeness to the emotion of anger or grief, dressing thoughts in fitting words" (*Confessions* 1.16–17). For a young student of rhetoric, the challenge was to feign written sentiment stylishly.

Along the road of his conversions, Augustine would discover better ways of acting on reading. Still, his critique of false images does not imply that all images should be banned from Christian teaching. In the garden (or Garden) that is remembered as the setting for his final turn toward God, Augustine sees not Christ but a figure of personified Continence. On one side, he imagines his "old mistresses," "vanities of vanities," and "violent habit" (8.11). On the other, he pictures "the chaste dignity of Continence, serene and cheerful without dissolution, coaxing decently." She gestures toward her "flocks of good examples." Augustine put the motions of her hands into words: "'Can't you do what these boys do, what these girls do?'" Augustine is ashamed to be attending to his old pleasures rather than her smiled invitation. He imagines that she now speaks, paraphrasing Paul: "Deafen yourself to your impure members on earth that they may be mortified" (after Col. 3:5). The rejection of false images is completed through true ones. Idolatrous playacting is overcome by a holy pantomime. The gospel speaks through bodily imagination to warn against the misuse of imagination. Alypius is not alone in wanting spectacle.

The book by Teresa of Ávila called *The Interior Castle* is sustained imagining that often becomes theater. Teresa is willing to make herself ridiculous in the excess of her performances if only she can catch her readers. She is, in that way, a more shameless teacher than Augustine.

Mobile Scenes

Teresa wrote the *Castle* after writing much else. She composed it in two bursts when she was in her early sixties. Outwardly she had dedicated herself to a controversial reform of religious life. Inwardly, she had experienced a sequence of visions, mental and physical. The most intense was the *transverberación*, the transfixion or—more literally—the piercing blow. (Bernini rendered that event for later viewers in a notoriously erotic statue. Whatever its attractions, the marble figure is not a subtle reading of the saint.) About five years before she wrote the *Castle*, Teresa's prayer scenes culminated in what she could only describe as a spiritual marriage.

The lessons Teresa learned in those secret scenes, she stages again for her community. In the *Castle*, the outermost frame of instruction shows the founder of a religious movement teaching its members. The book regularly addresses "sisters" and "daughters," titles that imply specific relations of learning. Her religious community has its rule or pattern of life, its daily liturgical practice, its roster of exemplary saints—both models and intercessors. There are living authorities as well, among whom Teresa holds first place. Inwardly, the community cultivates distinctive practices of prayer, about which Teresa will now offer remarkable advice through images that become tableaux and then participatory theater.

Her book goes by the English title *The Interior Castle*. Teresa calls it that at least once in the text, but she also refers to it as *Moradas*. (A manuscript copy of the work combines these two: *Moradas of the Interior Castle*.) When *morada* occurs within the text, some translators render it as "dwelling place." In other uses, the word means habitation or seat (of a bodily humor, a feudal lord, God). If you look to religious texts Teresa knew, or samples of speech she could have heard, you will find that *morada* regularly refers to sites or stages of spiritual ascent. It can be a hidden place for ascetical or spiritual practice. (In northern New Mexico, the chapels of *penitentes* are still called *moradas*.) Teresa's use of the word links a place to a time by dividing motion into stages. The *morada* locates an episode in learning. It is another name for a scene of instruction.

A *morada* is an artificial unit in Teresa's imagination of the fluid architecture of the interior castle. The challenge for her writing is to evoke a structure without betraying the placeless place of the soul's transformation. She dislocates the seven clusters of *moradas* that she enumerates. They shift positions. They multiply. There are millions of rooms, always moving in relation to the castle's center—which is the goal. On some pages, Teresa struggles to make her scene more vivid without reducing its dynamic complexity. Then she overturns it all to begin again. The reader should not become attached to any fixed configuration of learning—in time or space.

On my reading, the *Castle* is like an open-ended script for "immersive theater": performances in which the audience joins the actors in exploring—simultaneously, separately—various plot possibilities. If that comparison seems forced, you might at least compare Teresa's sketch of the moving scenes of divine teaching to Augusto Boal's models for "simultaneous dramaturgy," "image theater," and "forum theater."[1]

Homely Writing

The castle's shifting places are imitated by turns in Teresa's writing. Several times, for example, she notes that she treats something out of sequence. Other disclaimers about disorganization are verbal parallels to the twisting space she describes. Even her tendency to go on and on mimics the castle's multiplying rooms.

Teresa does tell a story: she moves from the lack of prayer to beginning prayer and discursive meditation, then through increasing spiritual candor and vulnerability, finally to spiritual betrothal and marriage. But Teresa complicates this plotline—and then digresses from it. She also puts the whole narrative under acknowledged limits of language. Teresa faces the challenge of inward description in homely images and "the language of women with each other."[2] She plays with and against the misogynistic stereotypes hurled at her. She concedes that caricatures of women's talk may indeed describe her penchant for examples and comparisons (*comparaciones*). She then flips the insult. Her concrete writing is a teaching device borrowed from divine instruction. Teresa's resort to homely comparisons copies God's pedagogy in at least three ways. It appeals to the love of beauty. It illustrates a proper use of imagination. It registers the paradoxes of spiritual teaching.

Beauty first. Teresa marvels at the castle. She cannot find comparisons enough for it. The castle is a pearl and a tree of life; the shimmering fountain within it, a shining sun. By such beauties, the soul is drawn to the royal chamber at the castle's center. They strengthen moral motivations: the soul cannot bear to offend God after seeing the ugliness of sin. Here, more extravagantly than in Bonaventure's *Itinerarium*, God educates through overwhelming attractions.

As Teresa stresses the power of beauty to lure, she reminds the reader of imagination's dangers. Our discursive efforts should be distinguished from God's gifts. She illustrates this—because images are required even in cautions about imagination—by describing two fountains, one fed by aqueducts, the other by springs. Aqueducts are built with ingenuity and labor. Springs produce water spontaneously, in unexpected places. Imagination often labors to construct vivid comparisons. Sometimes, unpredictably, beauties stream into the eye, over skin. This is the contrast between effort and grace—or the paradox of teaching under grace.

Learning Your Own Soul

Teresa's worries about imagination lead her to decipher the soul's capacities. Her lists of faculties are not catechetical answers for recitation; they are prompts to a practice of self-awareness. Teresa claims that she learned from experience how to distinguish faculties and where to locate them. She also reports encountering demonic deceit. The devil works particularly through the imagination, so weak heads with feverish imaginations get into trouble. Imagination spawns lizards that besiege the soul in the early stages of its journey. Lizards crawling over the skin: What more vivid figure could there be for distracting fancies?

Teresa's readers must learn to use their faculties without bending them against created nature. The practice of concentrating thoughts does not mean trying to stop thinking altogether, which is impossible. The task is rather to detach from thoughts and then to release them in suspended union with God. Long before that moment, readers must realize a fundamental ignorance of themselves. Some of those outside the castle will not discover a way in even though it lies as near as their own souls. So, Teresa imagines a brazier burning incense at the castle's center. You cannot see it, but you can smell the aroma. Our relation to our souls is something like that. We need to be guided—by the nose, if necessary. Or by our ears: Teresa imagines the divine call as a shepherd's whistle. Somehow the soul hears it. But how? And how does it teach the listening soul to enter the castle?

The reliability of spiritual instruction is a constant worry in Teresa's text. She complains that she simply cannot set forth the most important things. She cites the command under which she writes as her only excuse to keep writing. There are many mistakes in teaching and few insights. Experience is paramount. Without it, no reliable guidance for prayer is possible. But her own experience has changed over time—and with it her efforts. Each of her written works, it turns out, has been a *morada*, a temporary scene of instruction. The most vivid constructions of imagination are good for a season—because they reflect a time in the life of the teacher. I am not sure whether Teresa wishes that all her earlier works would disappear or whether she leaves them, with a resigned shrug, for whatever use they might still have.

Teresa treats herself as a source of knowledge and sometimes even of certainty—say, with respect to divine union. She displays her life as one example of divine pedagogy. She too becomes a "comparison" or "example." She is as candid about the difficulties of temptation or failure—lizard bites, malign choices at an advanced stage—as she is about the difficulty of finding one's way forward. There are millions of *moradas*, and the path through them is never a straight line. How could it be? The Spirit always moves.

The Lord's Teaching

Faced with these enigmas of spiritual counsel, it can be tempting to raise Teresa's book to the status of "mysticism" (a dubious elevation). We would effectively dismiss it by reserving it for mystics, saints, or (better) sainted mystics. That dismissal denies the intent and the effects of her writing. This is not a book for adepts about rare episodes. It is a guide for the beginner—and Teresa's reader always remains a beginner. There are many stages of approach to God. Progress is never assured: spiritual advancement brings underlying rebellion to the surface. Mature students carry still the basic vices, and beginners are sometimes swept along by the flowing spring.

Here, if not before, the very notion of ordered progress breaks apart. In the *Castle*, Teresa gradually replaces the official language of merit with that of divine gift or favor. How useful is it to read about favors? Reading will not bring them. Nothing a reader can do will compel their gift. God gives them according to God's free pedagogy. Still, there is this strong comfort: God is a bridegroom waiting at the center of a palace of gifts. What groom withholds gifts on the wedding day?

Teresa runs the risks of teaching through such comparisons because she remembers another teacher who spoke plainly, in domestic settings, using many comparisons and analogies. He recounted little scenes, more than a few about weddings. Within the system of gender types that Teresa inherits and reverses, Jesus taught as a woman would teach. When Teresa counsels her sisters, she imitates Jesus teaching his students—imitates his language, his settings, and his use of imagination.

If the gospel example is too exalted, there may be another way to reflect on these associations. According to the prevailing gender ideology, women are given to flights of fancy and endless chatter. They are also assigned to drudgery. Is imagination supposed to be their compensation for hard work? Or is there perhaps something to be learned about the relation of vivid images to languages for getting things done, for keeping life moving? What is called women's language is further appropriate for the education of children—because that is something else ideologically assigned to women. Of course, the church is supposed to be a household, and little children are those in it who move most by growing up.

John Bunyan,
Pilgrim's Progress

If ever a Christian book featured its anxiety about images, the book would be *Pilgrim's Progress*.[1] Yet the book produces enduring effects on English-speaking Protestants through two sorts of images: the fictions of its allegory and the illustrations added to its editions from early on. Both kinds of images press onto reader's memories. Here is one testimony, from a novel by Anthony Powell:

> Moreland said that, after his aunt read [*Pilgrim's Progress*] aloud to him as a child, he could never, even after he was grown-up, watch a lone figure draw nearer across a field, without thinking this was Apollyon come to contend with him. From the moment of first hearing that passage read aloud—assisted by a lively portrayal of the fiend in an illustration, realistically depicting his goat's horns, bat's wings, lion's claws, lizard's legs—the terror of that image, bursting out from an otherwise at moments prosy narrative, had embedded itself for all time in the imagination.[2]

An adult—late in life—recalls a childhood memory shared by an old friend some years before. The recollection shows how *Pilgrim's Progress* teaches across times. It also suggests that spiritual allegory can be overwhelmed by more literal illustrations.

The text of *Pilgrim's Progress* appeared in only two editions before illustrations were added. The third London edition carried Robert White's portrait of the author asleep—dreaming, as we do. A fifth London edition includes the first illustration of an incident in the book's allegory: the martyrdom of the character Faithful, at Vanity Fair.[3] The choice of topic may not be incidental: even Protestant readers suspicious of images were accustomed to illustrations of the final sufferings of their heroes. (Recall Foxe's *Book of Martyrs*.) From that one incident, the illustrations in *Pilgrim's Progress* multiplied—and changed according to successive tastes. We could judge that the allegory is doubled by the illustrations. Or we could worry that the illustrations undo the allegory by reducing it to a polemical tract. Over generations, illustrators and publishers have been considerably less worried than the author about teaching by images.

From Allegory to Illustration

On the title page of the first edition of the book's first part, before any engravings had been added, one word stands out as if it were illuminated or illustrated: "The Pilgrim's Progress from this world, to that which is to come: delivered under the Similitude of a DREAM . . ." The last word is set in large, embellished letters. It points in several directions. For example, the Bible tells of dreams that provide individual guidance, impel prophecy, or announce apocalypse. Ancient philosophical dreams are reinterpreted by Christian authors as cosmic patterns or ladders of spiritual ascent (famously, the dream of Scipio from Cicero's *De republica* 6). For other Christians, certain dreams foretell judgment and afterlife. (Dante's *Divine Comedy* can seem both a dream and a vision.) When Bunyan offers his book as the record of a dream, he claims some (thin) defense against prosecution for heresy. What is more important, he opens an inward space of instruction. As with Teresa's castle, everything shown in it is intended to teach. The device of a dream allows Bunyan to step around the problem of judging any particular person's salvation or damnation—election or reprobation—by external appearances. For this sleeping vision, captions are provided as if by God. Imagine a world in which everyone's deepest character is infallibly labeled for easy inspection.

Of course, dreams bring risks—and not only of mistaken judgment or deluded doctrine. The inward space of teaching opened by the book invites new images. Bunyan creates not only a geography but a sort of mythology, a supplement to Scripture. Though he takes pains to index his story to the Bible, filling the margins with citations, he still risks supplanting the Scriptures in imagination with this new text—of erecting narrative idols in front of scriptural stories. (Looking back to my quotation from Powell, I wonder whether Moreland's memories of the Christian Scriptures informed his adult experience quite so vividly as *Pilgrim's Progress* did. What does it mean to remember Bunyan better than the Bible?) It is no wonder that Bunyan begins with an "author's apology for his book."

The apology's chief topic is reliance on verbal allegory—not illustrations, which hadn't yet been added. The worries about allegory are never enumerated, but they seem to arise from the conviction that such a "method" or "style" is obscure—that it relies too much on darkness, shadow, mantling, feigning. Bunyan offers three replies to the worries. First, he says, just as a hunter or fisher will use any means to capture prey, so should an author seize the reader for Christian teaching. Bunyan's simile has gospel authority: Jesus promised to make his students fishers of other human beings. A second reply to the unstated objection against allegory makes the scriptural appeal more explicit: allegory is justified by its regular use in the Bible. The Law itself is set forth by type, shadow, metaphor, parable, figure, and similitude. Bunyan's third reply may be the most interesting. It suggests that human life itself is allegory. A reader will have at least as much trouble construing the lives around her as reading Bunyan. In fact, interpreting a book's allegory may be significantly easier than reading lives. Having offered these defenses, Bunyan takes a further step that almost elides the difference between allegory and illustration. He likens his allegory to a chalk drawing. (Chalk was valued in fine art drawing not only for shading or shadowing but also for its expressive lines.) *Pilgrim's Progress* is already a set of pictures when it consists only of words.

The connection of allegory to illustration runs through the book. Recall the episode inside the Interpreter's house. Here Christian, the protagonist pilgrim, must learn how to understand what he will see during the rest of his journey. He faces a long route across a landscape full of unexpected helps and deceptive temptations. His arrival at the heavenly gates will be aided by what he is taught here about how to read scenes. Interpreter's house offers lessons equally for Bunyan's reader—or for any Christian studying the Scriptures in order to make sense of the world.

It is striking, then, that the first thing the pilgrim sees in Interpreter's house is a portrait: "a Picture of a very grave Person. . . . [The figure] *had eyes lifted up to Heaven, the best of Books in its hand, the Law of Truth was written upon its lips, the World was behind its back*" (29). As so often, Christian is puzzled. (Our pilgrim shares with Jesus's disciples a tendency to befuddled astonishment. How could it be otherwise given what they see and hear? Should we then cultivate befuddlement in theological classrooms?) Interpreter, who serves as guide, explains: "The Man whose Picture this is, is one of a thousand, he can beget Children, Travel in birth with Children, and Nurse them himself when they are born." A standard reading takes this figure as the reliable (and so rare) Christian minister. I accept that reading. I add that the figure is equally a Christian teacher. The Pauline images of male mothering—which would be disconcerting if they weren't overly familiar—call to mind the steady patience of spiritual instruction. The portrait's main lesson is to be careful in trusting teachers, but it also suggests how much labor is required to beget, bear, and nurse beginners in faith. Paul writes, "I gave you milk, not solid food, for you were not yet ready for it. Indeed, you are still not ready" (1 Cor. 3:2). Bunyan affirms this lesson but does not represent it literally: the portrait does not show the "very grave Person" breast-feeding. That (biblical) interpretation is supplied only by Interpreter's words. We might attribute this to squeamishness about literalizing the Pauline comparison, but there is more. Within Bunyan's text (if not in its later illustrations), images are curiously mute until explained. They show and conceal simultaneously, more like clues than diagrams. After the portrait, Christian is shown tableaux or enactments. (A thoroughly modern Bunyan would insert video clips.) The second scene, after the portrait, depicts the room of the heart that needs to be swept by law and watered by gospel. Then there are two lads in chairs, Passion and Patience. In the fourth scene, the devil throws water on the fire of grace, which is restored through oil supplied by Christ. The pilgrim witnesses next a skirmish to enter the gates of the palace of heaven. In the sixth room, there is a professor in an iron cage, denied repentance—a warning against mere erudition. Finally, in the seventh room, the tableau shows a man terrified by a dream of the day of judgment. This is, within the book's frame, a dream within a dream—but also a reminder of the book's intended effect. Summarizing these scenes, I have collapsed the emblem and its caption, the tableaux and their program notes. Following Interpreter from room to room, Christian sometimes contributes an explanation. He does so especially with the two lads and the gates of heaven. In no case does Christian provide the entire account. Something must always be added by Interpreter or the actors in the scenes.

A reader of Teresa might be struck by several things. The sequence of rooms Christian sees is more orderly than the castle's *moradas*. The same might be said of Bunyan's whole landscape, which is both more static and less mysterious than Teresa's mobile, multiplying stages. A reader fresh from the *Interior Castle* might notice next that the House's images, while fixed, require explanation. They do not have the sensory immediacy of lizards, fountains, aromatic braziers, or subliminal whistles. Bunyan's scenes are not so much homely comparisons as riddling emblems in need of deciphering. If Teresa takes from Jesus the practice of plain teaching for domestic spaces, Bunyan copies the disciples' frequent bafflement at their master's parables. "What means this?"—that is Christian begging Interpreter for explanations, but it could just as well be the disciples after hearing a new parable. If he is an exemplary pilgrim, Christian is particularly inept at interpreting allegory.

A Certificate of Invisible Grace

From the author's apology on, the text of Pilgrim's Progress is filled with images (leaving aside, again, the added illustrations). What can all this teaching through images actually do for the protagonist or the reader? How does the telling of scenes help her progress? On Bunyan's understanding of grace, answers to these questions cannot be simple. Recall three points in the text: what "conversion" means, the continuing need of punishment or fear, and the undoing of the idea of pedagogical progress in the constant threat of damnation.

Christian's conversion does *not* occur when he abandons his family and flees his city to begin the pilgrimage. Nor is it a matter of giving outward signs of grace as he makes his uneven progress. Indeed, the pilgrim's conversion is not so much doing as avoiding. He is in constant peril, and the dangers do not lessen along the way. He makes no progress at all in that sense. Nor is there a clear series of stages by which—as in Dante—the soul approaches the vision of God. In *Pilgrim's Progress*, hell runs right up to the walls of heaven. This is what the dreamer realizes just before waking: "I saw that there was a way to Hell, even from the Gates of Heaven" (163). Whatever Christian learns, it is not a steady accumulation of better habits leading to some resistance against serious sin.

Does the character of Christian undergo anything like a progressive education? That may be the wrong question. Consider the last few pages of the text. The reader is shown the pilgrim's repetition of sins and errors up to the last minute. Our hero almost drowns in the river before the gates of the heavenly city. He has also quite forgotten the crucial text entrusted to him. In the end, this "Certificate, which [he] had received in the beginning," is more important than any lessons culled along the way (161). The character called Ignorance is damned for arriving at the gates without a certificate; all his journeying did not supply the indispensable requirement for salvation. Fortunately, a certificate was given to Christian by one of the "shining ones" as he stood weeping before the cross: "the third . . . gave him a Roll with a Seal upon it" (38). The contents of the roll are not further described. They cannot be. In fact, a reader could be forgiven for forgetting about the "Roll" until it is demanded by the keepers of the heavenly gate. The narrative techniques that Bunyan uses to portray Christian's pilgrimage cannot say much about what is required for its happy conclusion.

Some commentators supply a technical account of what the certificate represents in Bunyan's theology. I prefer to see it as a cipher for the many paradoxes of education under grace. Bunyan's book begins by justifying the use of allegory as a teaching device. Bunyan does teach, on page after page of a richly imagined story, bolstered by citations to scriptural texts (many of them also stories) and ornamented by increasingly specific illustrations. Still, Bunyan cannot give the reader a certificate. A claim to confer it by his teaching would be blasphemy.

You might conclude that Bunyan's practice contradicts his doctrine. It would be fairer to say that he is willing to teach without having to know in advance the outcomes. (That uncertainty applies to all teaching.) The use of so many devices of imagination must count in Bunyan's theology as mostly wasted effort. It may, under God's providence, provide some small consolation to the saints. Still, the decisive teaching is God's—or, rather, the important gift is God's alone to give. Bunyan believes that it is more like a certificate than a lesson. You would not guess that from the urgent imaginings of his scenes of instruction.

11

The Use and Abuse of Imagination

The importance of images is enshrined in Christian Scriptures (Gen. 1:27; Col. 1:15) and affirmed as doctrine (from the human as *imago Dei* to the Son as image of the Father). If some Christians have rejected representational art forms, none have done away entirely with imaginative means of instruction (nor could they). Christians in the majority have endorsed and sponsored many varieties of religious art. You could write a history of Christian education through church iconography and architecture; another from select devotional images, in public or private spaces, displayed and worn.

Text-based theological teaching sometimes uses Christian art only as illustration—like putting slides up to relieve a boring lecture. This can imply that words are indubitably the truth of theology, while a painting or sculpture is at best a pretty supplement. But images are more intimately linked to theology than that. They reenact God's incarnate instruction. The fate of Christian theology, whether as pedagogy or inquiry, is entangled with the fate of images, the ones it uses and the ones that compete with it.

Transforming Narrative

Theology depends on images because human beings learn through their senses. The risk of idolatry arises only when we count as complete what we so partially see, hear, taste, touch, or smell. (If idolatry is often described as a distorted visual relation, any sense can suffer it.) Since God was willing to take flesh to teach flesh, there can be no final objection against using the senses in Christian theology. The incarnation justifies what creation should have made plain: rightly used, images and other artworks are integral parts of human teaching about the highest things.

It would be better, in fact, if Christian teachers abandoned the dichotomy of text and image. Too often discussions of idolatry focus on single artworks extracted from their intended settings. The mistake is encouraged by modern museums. The appropriate setting for Christian artworks is liturgy and private devotion, pilgrimage and procession, musical celebration and progressive meditation. Recognizing these narrative contexts, both Teresa and Bunyan are typical of older traditions. Their tableaux take place within sequences. Indeed, both books teach their readers how to convert the stories of the Scriptures or the lives of the saints into linked scenes for present instruction.

The relation of images to imagined narratives is particularly important in moral transformation—which is the central preoccupation of both Teresa and Bunyan, though in different ways. Each book tells a journey. The journey is sketched in a sequence of scenes. Passing through the scenes by imagination aids the pilgrimage. Both Teresa and Bunyan mean to assist the journey by telling it from imagination to imagination.

Imagined Futures

For most of Teresa's readers, the royal chamber at the center of the imagined castle is far away. So too is Mount Zion, which Bunyan's Christian seeks. On Teresa's account, no clear path leads to the chamber—though there may be some faint scent of perfume lingering this far out. Imagination is required to picture the destination, to persevere in hoping for it. So too with Bunyan, under a different economy of grace: the one thing required—

within the imagined story—is to reach the gates of the heavenly city with your certificate. But there are so many temptations, distractions, deviations! It is hard to continue when you are mired in despair or beaten by giants or confronted by towering demons coming at you across the field. Imagination must evoke the end repeatedly as consolation along the way.

If imagination brings the promised future near, it also helps to open a way toward it—so far as any human action can. In Christian scenes of instruction, as in liturgy, possibilities for living otherwise are put before those who participate. These possibilities are imagined forms for the promised fulfillments of grace. The completion of Christian life appears first as utopian fiction. How important it becomes, then, to write fictions convincingly.

Theology in an Age of Mechanical Reproduction

Because theology depends on images in these and other ways, any significant change in the prevailing economy of images will affect it. A disruption in that economy may foreclose certain theological uses of image—and forms for Christian teaching along with them.

Most human groups are now undergoing unprecedented changes in the production and circulation of images. Old assumptions about the "normal" exposure to images no longer hold. We inhabit visual environments saturated with pictures of unrivaled vividness, electronic voices and noises, engineered smells. This is sometimes described, rightly, as a new economy of attention. It is, more precisely, an economy of engineered distraction, which quickly exhausts both words and sensations.

Faced with such cultural disruptions, teachers of theology must expect trouble when they appeal to imagination. The challenges cannot be met by shaming students into spending less time on social networks or avoiding pornographic sites. (I use "pornography" in its ordinary and quite loose sense. It is not hard to argue that an hour of prime-time advertising blights human living more than an hour of filmed copulation.) Nor is the cultural disruption adeptly handled by copying the new image regimes. Efforts to catch up will fail. On the one hand, no school of theology can afford to compete with the most intoxicating media platforms. (Our special effects always look cheaper—because they are.) On the other hand, the study of theology requires mental practices that are the opposite of those cultivated by modern media. (The assumption of any serious teaching is that you can sustain attention and accumulate what you notice.) The salvation of an instant often needs long preparation. Part of the work of the theological teacher now is to restore the student's capacity for attentive imagining.

A more adequate theological response to our present chaos of sounding images would be to discover their transfiguration. After some years of saying this, I am still not sure what I mean by the phrase. Sometimes I worry that I have become my own parody—like Chekhov's character, Treplev, who declaims, "We must have new forms" (*Seagull*, act 1). But then I fall back on my core conviction: in teaching, as also in writing, form and content are finally inseparable. We do need new forms to enliven the good news. We can set out to follow the latest fashions or to ignore them, but either way we will encounter in our hearers or readers current cultures of representation.

My best guess is that we need new forms for handling uneven excess—boom and bust, boredom and overstimulation, too many colors and never enough. I have begun to liken this new form to what we call "baroque." I recall something that Susan Sontag wrote about Walter Benjamin: "His style of thinking and writing, incorrectly called aphoristic, might better be called freeze-frame baroque. The style was torture to execute. It was as if each sentence had to say everything. . . . Something like the dread of being stopped prematurely lies behind these sentences as saturated with ideas as the surface of a baroque painting is jammed with movement."[1] The intended effect is described by Benjamin himself in Sheaf N of the *Arcades-Project*, under the rubric "Waking": "It's not that the past casts its light on the present. Rather an image is that in which the Then and the Now flash together into a constellation. In other words: image is dialectics at a standstill." But I then recall the famous remark in Benjamin's "Theses on History" (more correctly, "On the Concept of History"), number 7: "There is no document of culture [*Kultur*] which is not at the same time one of barbarism."[2]

The constellations of our theological baroque must include records of horror—not least, the ones authored by Christendom. Any night's news can project fresh atrocities. Some days, the images I most want to forget are the ones held up in churches for veneration.

> **Exercise:** Draft a syllabus for teaching "Introduction to Christian Theology" that assigns only images of various kinds, including feature films. Now rewrite it using just the kinds of images available a hundred years ago—a thousand, if you know that medieval world better. How might you wean students from skimming today's most dazzling of images without committing the heresy of rejecting images altogether?
>
> **Alternate form of the exercise:** Build in imagination your own version of Interpreter's house. What are the indispensable acts of interpreting images in our present cultural circumstances? What is the present task in reeducating *perception*?

4

Children

C. S. Lewis, The Lion, the Witch and the Wardrobe

Pick up a list of Christian books in English ranked by volumes sold. If you set aside the Bible, official prayer books, and *Pilgrim's Progress*, you reach *The Lion, the Witch and the Wardrobe* almost immediately. Sales figures provide no indication of quality or religious merit. (Other books atop the sales lists are frightening.) Still, the numbers can lead us to reflect on *The Lion*'s wide appeal, at least part of which has been to children. One of the distinctive features of religious language is how early it reaches many people and with what magical authority. Whenever I teach Lewis, I begin by asking how many in the room encountered him when they were children. The results can be surprising. One graduate student, a remarkably astute reader, had been raised in an Orthodox Jewish community. She was startled to discover that *The Lion* was considered Christian allegory. Her school had assigned it as suitable ethical instruction. You might think this story idiosyncratic, but it can still suggest a simple experiment. I urge you to perform it, if only for ten minutes.

> **Experiment:** Leaving aside Scriptures or prayer books, what sorts of books stand out in your childhood memories as religious or spiritual, especially if you did not have a religious upbringing? What were the *actual* inspirations for your childhood theology? So far as you can, set aside offi-

cial versions of the world that various adults were trying to inculcate in you and that you never really took in.

On *The Lion*'s first dust jacket, the subtitle reads "A Story for Children."[1] The publisher may have added the phrase as a caution to readers of Lewis's earlier books. In the years just before, he had published novels or allegories (*That Hideous Strength*, *The Great Divorce*), a first version of *Miracles*, a study of Charles Williams's elaborate poetry, and a book of lectures. Readers were alerted: *The Lion* is for children. Or so the cover says.

The genre alert is ambivalent. Long before Freud—I mean, before his scandalous claims about infant pleasures—children's stories were filled with desire, conflict, and violence. Recall the grisly horrors of "Little Red Riding Hood" or "Hansel and Gretel." Remember too how often religious education recites violent stories to children. (At five or six, I was unable to sleep for several nights after seeing a pious film on the sixteenth-century Japanese martyrs. It was screened at the parish church of the Mexican village in which my mother lived.) Still, and without simplifying too much, I distinguish two readings of *The Lion*. The first reading, the most obvious, takes that cover at its word when it promises "a book for children." The second reading sees Lewis offering an alternate, more consoling catechesis for adults. The two readings are not exclusive. In fact, the second might well depend on the first, since part of the book's power to console adults could depend on retrieving a genre from childhood.

Lewis hints at this sequence of readings in his preface. He addresses his goddaughter, Lucy Barfield (whose father had helped Lewis's own conversion in adulthood): "I wrote this story for you, but when I began it I had not realized that girls grow quicker than books. As a result you are already too old for fairy tales, and by the time it is printed and bound you will be older still. But some day you will be old enough to start reading fairy tales again" (5). Note that he speaks of "fairy tales," not stories for children. A fairy tale is a kind of instruction that can become both useful and delightful at widely spaced ages or between the times. Indeed, Lewis elsewhere connects fairy tales with mythmaking, perhaps "one of the greatest arts."[2]

Children's Stories

The Lion, the Witch and the Wardrobe is a story *about* children. They are its main characters—and its chief learners. The plot features their deeds in a hidden world, Narnia, where they act out a drama of good and evil. The book also tells how they learn the relation of that world to this.

The novel presents these protagonists in ways that other children are supposed to recognize. The reader is introduced to them by their first names, because those are the names children use. The characters are described by family relations and rivalries. As it turns out, they have been sent away from their families—their ordinary lives—because of a war. Before they enter the wardrobe that opens on the hidden world, they are already in a separate place. It is marked off from the realm of adults by the first line: "Once there were four children . . ." (9).

The Lion is told *to* children. It is filled with examples of direct address, often at moments of especially intense feeling or when something important must be explained. Feelings are named and approved. Here is the first description of the Stone Table, site of the novel's central action: "It was a great grim slab of grey stone supported on four upright stones. It looked very old; and it was cut all over with strange lines and figures that might be the letters of an unknown language. They gave *you* a curious feeling when you looked at them" (117 [emphasis added]). Religious ritual invites participants to take a position within a scene. This children's book teaches appropriate feelings the way that a liturgy teaches Christian life. *The Lion* also uses direct address to strengthen the sense of complicity with its readers. For example, the narrator abbreviates a list of monsters with the remark, "and other creatures whom I won't describe because if I did the grown-ups would probably not let you read this book" (140).

The conventions of children's literature allow Lewis to emphasize scenes of instruction. (Children are supposedly not embarrassed to be taught.) The narrator is chatty and opinionated—that is, didactic. He (could we imagine this voice as she or they?) frequently interrupts the telling. Sometimes he offers opinions—say, about the tastiness of freshwater fish. At other moments, he underlines differences between Narnia and our world. When Beaver makes a grammatical mistake, the narrator adds, "that is how beavers talk when they are excited; I mean, in Narnia—in our world they usually don't talk at all" (100).

The narrator also cautions that his telling of the story is only one among many. "Lucy came forward. [Father Christmas] gave her a little bottle of what looked like glass (but people said afterward that it was made of diamond) and a small dagger" (102). Behind all tellings, there is a mysterious reality that no single telling can exhaust. Something similar appears from time to time in the canonical Gospels: "Jesus performed many other signs in the presence of his students, which are not recorded in this book" (John 20:30). If we take *The Lion* seriously, we should be puzzled by assertions that the approved Scriptures "[contain] all things necessary to salvation" or that some historic creeds constitute "the sufficient statement of the Christian faith."[3] The children are taught differently: the only thing necessary for their being rescued is love, and no single story in a human language can capture it.

Teaching in Narnia

The simplicity of Lewis's story is not just stylistic. The story unfolds in high ethical contrast. The struggle between good and evil is made especially clear—as sharp as in *Pilgrim's Progress*, if not so heavy-handed. The characters are rendered in primary colors as types. If they don't carry Bunyan's allegorical names, they certainly illustrate virtue and vice. They show as clearly possibilities for reformation. A reader knows that something is wrong with Edmund early on, from the moment when fatigue makes him cruel to Lucy. Still, even Edmund never loses his moral sense:

"deep down inside him he really knew that the White Witch was bad and cruel" (85). A reader witnesses his moral reeducation—or repentance—across the book.

The clarity of the moral lessons increases with narrative exclusions. There are no sexual relations in this book and, of course, no permanent triumph of evil. Other exclusions are odder. It isn't hard to find lines where moral lessons are indistinguishable from rules for (a fantasy of?) British "middle-class" life, with its settled relations of gender and class. Fortunately, there is no need to defend the whole of Lewis's instruction in order to learn from his best scenes.

The book gives mixed moral instruction, then, but more famously a Christian education. Let me sample the allusions, to show both their frequency and, in some cases, their subtlety. To begin at the beginning: Learning about Aslan is like getting "good news" (76), an evangel or gospel. Reports say that Aslan is "the son of the great Emperor-beyond-the-Sea," God in heaven (77). The Stone Table is an altar on which Jesus's last supper is repeated as Aslan's voluntary submission to sacrifice by the evil Witch. That deed overrules the Deep Magic engraved on the firestones of Secret Hill, which is the law given to Moses on Mount Sinai. (Aslan's new deed is greater than the old law.) The night before Aslan's sacrifice, Susan and Lucy are unable to keep watch with him—just as Jesus's students fell asleep in the garden of Gethsemane. Aslan shorn and trussed for slaughter is Jesus in his passion—and the lamb led to the slaughter in Isaiah 53:7. Aslan then rises from the dead: "At that moment they heard from behind them a loud noise—a great cracking, deafening noise as if a giant had broken a giant's plate" (148). This is the breaking open of Jesus's tomb.

How many of these references are children supposed to recognize? That may be the wrong question. Perhaps the book works by making certain sorts of stories probable or familiar, imaginable. The allusions in *The Lion*, recognized or not, prepare younger readers for hearing the gospel later on. They activate capacities that will be needed for discerning religious realms beyond scientific reduction and managerial control.

Innovating in Narnia

Contented with their allegorical discoveries, Christian readers of Lewis sometimes stop short. They miss his other accomplishments. *The Lion* doesn't just repeat old tales as remote preparation for later faith. It recasts the stories it tells. To put it in jargon: Lewis "does theology" while re-presenting the Christian message. Perhaps two examples can show this.

Mr. Beaver remarks, in an apparent aside: "When you meet anything that's going to be human and isn't yet, or used to be human once and isn't now, or ought to be human and isn't, you keep your eyes on it and feel for your hatchet" (79). This is a robust affirmation of human reality—of the goodness of creation, a theologian might say. It is also a reference to the idiosyncratic theology of another of Lewis's friends, Charles Williams. In Williams's 1937 novel *Descent into Hell*, the main agent of evil is a chameleon being who mimics human happiness—indeed, human love and desire. Succumbing to that mimicry begins damnation.

Another example of Lewis's theological innovation is the scene of Aslan bringing Peter to the fullness of repentance for the harshness that drove Edmund away: "Aslan said nothing either to excuse Peter or to blame him but merely stood looking at him with his great unchanging eyes. And it seemed to all of them that there was nothing to be said" (120). Some scenes of instruction work most powerfully not by multiplying words but by the silence of mutual recognition. The point is reinforced a few pages later, as Edmund is forgiven of his much graver crimes. The children watch at a distance as Aslan and Edmund walk together. "There is no need to tell you (and no one ever heard) what Aslan was saying, but it was a conversation which Edmund never forgot." As the others approach, Aslan says to them, "Here is your brother . . . and—there is no need to talk to him about what is past" (128). The inmost scene of instruction—the healing of souls—is accomplished in an intimate, unreportable conversation.

We have been moving for a while now into the second reading

of *The Lion*—the reading that emphasizes how far this is a book for adults that uses means supposedly devised for children. Under the stress of Reformation polemics, but especially after the Enlightenment, Christian theology has been deprived of some powerful genres. Choosing to write in what is supposedly a children's genre, Lewis rehabilitates kinds of Christian speech surrendered for efficient polemic or intellectual authority.

The Lion shows that the world is bigger than the daily routines of busy adults or the devices of modern engineering and marketing. Lewis's Professor, the owner of the house in which the children have come to live, insists on intellectual humility, unflinching truthfulness, and the inscrutability of reality. By contrast, and before his moral recovery, Edmund demands simple certainty. For Lewis—as for his friends, Barfield and Williams—one way to resist a narrowing of moral vision is to treat as urgently real some of what modernity dismisses as prescientific fiction. Readers who stress the Christian allegory of *The Lion* sometimes forget Lewis's audacity in rehabilitating other figures of folktale or myth. Aslan appears surrounded by Dryads and Naiads, centaurs, and other "pagan" entities. The Queen's army contains a remarkable mix of legendary beings. The Queen herself is born from Adam and Lilith, who—we are told—descended from jinn and giants. (The interest in Lilith is another reference to Williams's *Descent into Hell*.) When Lewis fuses mythologies, he suggests how much of reality is omitted by current science. Lewis risks associating the Gospels with fairy tales to say, "Look how you must open your mind, your imagination, to hear the good news."

Many young Christians learn the gospel story about Jesus welcoming other children, long ago. Drawings of the encounter stare down from stained glass windows and its lessons echo in hymns ("Jesus loves the little children"). We usually take the story as a charter for religious education. Listen to it again. In Mark's version, some children are brought to Jesus for a blessing (Mark 10:13–16). When his students try to block their way (to protect the master, to get more time for themselves?), Jesus gets angry.

He orders them to let the children approach: "anyone who will not receive the kingdom of God like a little child will never enter it." Whatever else Lewis is doing with his books "for children," he is trying to work out the implications of that verse for every teaching of Christian theology.

13

Octavia Butler,
Parable of the Sower

Octavia Butler's *Parable of the Sower* is a novel with a gospel title that describes the rise of a new religion after Christianity's (future?) failure.[1] While no preface specifies its audience, the book is usually classed as "science fiction" and so consigned to adolescents or adults stuck in teen fandom. In these and other ways, Butler's novel comes *after* Lewis. It raises acute questions about the present survival of Christian teaching.

Like *The Lion*, Butler's novel is the first in a series of books, called Parable or Earthseed. I select features of the single book without trying to account for the rest. I'm drawn by its effort to perform life-giving teaching again, from the beginning, for those growing up. That is one reason why *Parable of the Sower* adopts a supposedly popular genre to respond to present religious crises. (Imagine the genre to which a finely educated Athenian poet would have consigned the Gospel of Mark on first reading—assuming he was able to tolerate the style for more than a few lines.) At the same time, *Parable* claims to connect its writing to the need for new Scriptures. It argues that Christian teaching has stopped working—not because it has been disproved by philology, neurobiology, or world history, but because it no longer saves our present.

The Scenes of "Science Fiction"

The mass appeal of science fiction has been part of its camouflage. Often discounted as cheap entertainment, it has been allowed to take up risky political, ethical, or religious topics. Samuel Delany cautions against falsely romanticizing the "freedom" of science fiction. The freedom, he reminds us, came along with poor pay, shoddy business practices, and lack of recognition.[2] Still, Delany's own work proves how deeply science fiction explores topics prohibited elsewhere. Butler doubles the genre's freedom by seeming to dismiss it. "I write about people who do extraordinary things. It just turned out that it was called science fiction."[3]

Parable of the Sower acknowledges its likely label. Butler's protagonist-narrator, Lauren, mentions science fiction at several points. In one passage, she contrasts the conventional genre expectations with the (fictional?) reality around her. "My grandmother left a whole bookcase of old science fiction novels. The company-city subgenre always seemed to star a hero who outsmarted, overthrew, or escaped 'the company.' I've never seen one where the hero fought like hell to get taken in and underpaid by the company. In real life, that's the way it will be. That's the way it is" (123–24). At one level, her reflection on the "old" genre calls for politically realistic science fiction. At another, the teasing about genre innovation—or *Parable*'s preoccupation with its own writing—both shields and complicates the text's frankly religious teaching.

Parable of the Sower speaks urgently to an apocalyptic present. The ravaged future is a common theme in science fiction, as Lauren admits. It is in fact a subgenre—that is, a form of address to a reader's established expectations. More: Apocalyptic is an old scriptural genre, not least in Judaism and Christianity. It has gained new popularity for Christian readers in the United States during recent decades. (The novels in the Left Behind series are reported to have sold more than 65 million copies. When I last checked, they had spawned several movies, an album, and a video game.) In both its old and new forms, apocalyptic writing registers a moment of acute cultural anxiety more visceral than Tillich's. It can foretell the disruptive return of old divinities fulfilling their scriptures—or the appearance of new divinities bearing text. One genre analogy to Butler's novel is Nietzsche's *Zarathustra*, which narrates the life of a teacher who flees collapsing Christendom to proclaim new rites atop a wilderness mountain. *Parable of the Sower* is Zarathustra in LA. Oh, and the prophet is now a black teenager.

The End of Christianity

"At least three years ago, my father's God stopped being my God. His church stopped being my church. And yet, today, because I'm a coward, I let myself be initiated into that church. I let my father baptize me in all three names of that God who isn't mine any more. My God has another name" (7).

Though Lauren's loss of Christian faith—her evangelical disenchantment—is the plot's pivot, it is not easily explained. She rejects childhood Christianity in part because it is a "mythology or mysticism or magic" that depends on "supernatural authority figures" (217, 219). Her new religion, Earthseed, grows from critical observation of the epochal shifts around her. Another complaint against Christianity is moral. Alarmed by troubles in the small neighborhood, Lauren's father preaches the Ten Commandments, with special emphasis on stealing. Somewhat later, she recalls the same passage as she steals to survive. Lauren rejects Christianity because it is unlivable. Patriarchal Christianity fails at largest scale because it cannot save itself from its collusion in destroying our planet. Lauren's favorite book in the Christian Bible is *Job*. That strange story of unmotivated suffering is the one section of the Scriptures that rings true as things disintegrate.

In *Parable of the Sower*, the succession of gods is generational. Of course, the book mixes old and new gods: in families, generations overlap. Quotations from the Christian Bible are scattered through this book, as are summaries of Christian sermons. The book's title refers to a New Testament story that is quoted at the novel's end. (A reader might conclude that Butler has written a commentary on that one parable by rewriting the gospel around it.) There are other references throughout to dislocated Christian symbols. The shaved and painted addicts of the drug "pyro" resemble devils manipulating hellfire. Tyrannical corporations are Pharaoh as overlord of the captive Israelites. The smoky firestorm that passes around the side of Lauren's small band during their flight is the column of cloud and fire leading Israel out of Egypt. The sharing of food that is so central to building trust could be another Eucharist, as the decisive moment of making community on the beach might seem another baptism. Butler is no less indebted to Christian materials than is Nietzsche in *Zarathustra* or Lewis in the Narnia books—but not in the same way.

The Huntington Library has posted a page of notes that Butler wrote to herself when working on *Parable of the Sower*.[4] Some of the jottings are typical reminders. "More heat & dust & thirst & stench & misery & fire." Followed by: "They must *see* the *sick* & *dying along the road*—like downtown LA only worse." Something else is written across the top of the page. "She [Lauren] is hagridden. Earthseed is Positive Obsession. It will *never* let go." And again, in pink: "The religion, EARTHSEED, is first, last, and foremost—*Goal*, *Whip*, and *Sustenance*." Whip is a recollection of slavery. For Lauren, presumed to be a descendant of slaves, writing Earthseed is a whip between goal and sustenance: she is driven from the failed religious past into the spoken/written religious future.

The Dream of a New Bible

Butler's *Parable* claims to disclose a new God. The author of these scriptures—the fictional author of the diary entries that make up the novel—stands outside dying traditions. Lauren is not just American, but Californian; she is young; she is black—attuned to racial differences and the legacies of slavery. She is an unlikely prophet or evangelist for any Establishment. (Weren't they all?) The novel quotes a "scripture" that is written as poetry. Once Lauren is asked whether the notebook she carries is poetry. "'A lot of it isn't very poetical,' I said. 'But it's what I believe, and I've written it as well as I could.' I showed him four verses in all—gentle, brief verses that might take hold of him without his realizing it and live in his memory without his intending that they should. Bits of the Bible had done that to me, staying with me even after I stopped believing" (199). Lauren searches for memorable verse that will rival the force of the old Christian scenes without imposing chains.

Or consider the genre of her diary. *Parable* is the spiritual autobiography of a religious founder. It is mostly narrated in the first person. We have in direct speech not only fragments of a scripture, but the narrative of how and why it is being written. Again, the novel is a set of writing notes for a new Bible. They register struggles to find language for what must be said, but they resist despair over the project of writing itself. What gives Lauren the liberty and confidence to write divinity plainly? One answer: she retells the exodus of Israel from Egypt as the underground railroad on another coast—the dream of escape from a slaveholding South to the free North (which means, a place where life has to be built from nothing). Lauren gains her capacity to write on her dangerous journey to hard liberty. In writing, she escapes the coercion of sweating for other masters.

Lauren is the importunate widow of the parable that she quotes (134, with reference to Luke 18:1-8). She has an insistent confidence that some different future can be called forth by writing and teaching. Her first insight is that God is change. The effort in the rest of her writing is to convey creative energy. She names the new idea or philosophy or religion Earthseed after working in the garden. Her writing does not fix or canonize. When Lauren tells her partner Bankole the essentials of the new teaching, he replies that it too will change as it spreads. A reader sees how that change might go when the novel describes Lauren's group in conversation about the new teaching. The conversation feels "almost like church" (294)—or like what church might have been in a less oppressive history of Christianity. Living teaching: the prolonged adolescence of a revelation.

14

Education and Resistance

If there are continuities between Lewis and Butler, the contrasts are sharp. In *The Lion*, children from a world at war join battle in another place and time to restore the rule of a Christlike figure. His restoration confirms and conforms to old scriptures. In *Parable*, a young woman not far beyond childhood leads an exodus from cities that have declared unconcealed war on their own citizens. She teaches a new religion as she begins to compose its scripture. The novel ends in a budding community that looks forward to something as yet unseeable.

The two books are separated by another sort of contrast. It is not so clear-cut as the difference between ideal children and real adolescents—though there is something of that. It has more to do with Aslan's success as a teacher in obvious contrast with the failure of Lauren's father. If Lewis's children join Aslan's cause to flourish, Lauren must reject her father's Christianity and flee his home to survive. Side by side, the two books show the complications of conversion and resistance.

I raise these issues in books about children and adolescents because they are particularly poignant there. The relations of teachers and students are often compared to family bonds. In the Gospels, those relations make new families. When Jesus's mother and brothers appear outside the house where he is teaching, he refuses their claims. "'Who is my mother, and who are my brothers?' And stretching out his hand to his learners (*tous mathētas*), he said, 'Here are my mother and my brothers!'" (Matt. 12:48-49). The community that seeks God's teaching displaces the biological family. What does that imply for relations of power among learners?

Abuse

It is hard to pose the question without thinking of recent scandals involving sexual abuse by ordained ministers. The abuse of children and adolescents in Christian institutions is horrifying. It began centuries ago and still continues, in part because it is so regularly denied and concealed. Still, sexual assault is not the only abuse of Christian teaching authority. Nor is it the only way destructive patterns from biological families carry over into the new "family" of Christian instruction.

Christian formation is invariably confused with the delights and sufferings of childhood when one is raised in a Christian home. In the same way, a Christian classroom fuses the gospel with more mundane practices of discipline and reward. If Sunday school lessons are enforced by beating or ridicule, the bruises and shames get added to the gospel proclamation. If a seminary classroom is driven mainly by prospects of preferment, the gospel becomes job training.

No policy revisions or mandated mini-courses can abolish these tyrannies. School boards may prohibit corporeal punishment and discourage bullying (they should), but human cruelty will find other ways to insinuate itself. Rather than pouring our energy into fantasies of perfect prevention, we might better concede the risks of teaching and consider how to heal (as best we can) its unpreventable abuses—trusting here too in more than our own efforts. If the unpredictability of grace sometimes undoes human efforts at orderly pedagogy, it also reassures us that our failures are not only ours to correct.

Powerful Teaching

Here is what I understand of the paradox of power in teaching. The gifts, arts, and techniques that produce transformation can also inflict serious harms. There is no way to separate the two potentialities. A charismatic teacher is always at risk of becoming a demagogue. A spiritual counselor who elicits trust to form souls can abuse that trust to deform them. Of course, the risks are not all on the side of teaching. Some students confuse desire for the persona of the teacher with the person behind it. Some teachers prey on that confusion; some students cultivate it.

Precautions can be taken. The teacher should highlight and observe her limits, especially when a student wants to ignore them. Pedagogical authority can be distributed within a community to prevent unbalanced relationships with a single faculty member. The sequence of instruction can propose a series of transfers from one relation to another. And so on. The best devices help in many settings for most students. Still, no set of regulations can eliminate all the risks of teaching for transformation. The gentlest, most guarded teaching attracts some students almost irresistibly. Transformation depends on that attraction. The only way to prevent attraction altogether is to restrict teaching to the impersonal transfer of affectless information. Some classrooms do succeed at that. In that success, they fail.

Adjusting regulations isn't the only reason for talking about pedagogical power. Teaching is one of the basic forms of human relation. We can learn from it what we are and what we are not. It is imperative to distinguish biological family from learning community. To say this in Christian terms: we discourage abusive teaching when we remember that the kingdom is not *my* family. It is supposed to displace both the pride and the possessiveness of "blood." In Lewis's story, Aslan is not the children's father. He is a lion. Even the Professor in whose house they live is not their father. Their actual parents are far away, beyond the borders of the book. If Aslan cares for the children, if they learn to love him, these relations are not literally familial. They depend rather on participation in a shared truth owned by none of them—not even Aslan. In Butler's *Parable*, more strongly, Lauren experiences Earthseed as a transformative truth that is hers to teach but neither to possess nor control. It grows as she talks and writes. It will continue to grow as it passes to others.

For all the care that a writer may lavish on a scene of instruction, the scene becomes effective when it goes beyond its design. The strongest scenes work not by saying "Become like me," or "Come join us," but "Enter into this, which exceeds us both."

Resistance

Michel Foucault frequently reminds his readers that each form of power elicits its own kinds of resistance. He sometimes illustrates this with a story about Christian structures in the European Middle Ages. As he traces the institutionalization of pastoral power, he notices the emergence of five "counter-conducts."[1] An adequate account of Christian institutions must include these five as much as the dominant institutions. They are not external effects of pastoral power. They arise within it.

The notion of counter-conduct can help to reconceive the complexity of relations in teaching. When teaching is powerful, it produces resistance. The resistance shouldn't be dismissed as dullness or disobedience. Some kinds of resistance do show where teaching has gone astray. But other kinds augur an emerging future. Still others prepare better exercises of Christian freedom. Instead of bewailing resistance, or trying to squelch it, we might think how to welcome it into a pedagogy that no human owns.

Jesus's saying about becoming like children remains. If we should resist the pretensions and abuses of human teachers, we are told to approach Jesus as children—not as subjects of enhanced surveillance or rights-bearing possessors of approved identities. To approach a teacher as a child requires some combination of trust, humility, and affection—held together by dependence or need. The most generous and the most damaging human teachings both try to reach that need by activating desire.

Exercise: Call up your fondest memories of your favorite teaching. How would you describe the emotions those memories draw from you? Try writing them down in five or ten minutes (no longer). Did it embarrass you to do that? How would it feel to describe them to another student of the same teacher? To one of your colleagues? Would you consider it appropriate to share them with one of your own students? If you worry about sharing them, do you also worry about trying to re-create them?

Exercise: What kinds of necessary resistance do you encounter to your teaching? Does it hurt you or scare you? Do you resent it? Could you imagine beginning to encourage it?

5

BARRIERS

15

Johannes Climacus (with the Assistance of Søren Kierkegaard), Philosophical Crumbs

Octavia Butler's *Parable* presents a future in which life-giving scenes of instruction have moved beyond Christian churches and failed families. What she describes is more than a dystopian future. It is an ever-present need for reform—in teaching as much as in other parts of church life. To say the obvious: earlier writers have also reproached the dissipation of Christian teaching while offering radical alternatives. Some agree with Butler in describing how they found a decisive scene of instruction unexpectedly—in the world outside the church gates, in a book not labeled as theology.

Consider, for example, a slim volume entitled *Philosophical Scraps* or *Crumbs*.[1] It is *not* a book of theology. The title plainly identifies it as philosophy, though of an odd sort. It is not the System, which any serious philosophy of course aspires to be. Only scraps. Perhaps not even a book after all. Just pieces, early drafts or late remnants—which you should expect to scatter when you try to hold them.

That won't do. We are getting muddled. Let's start over by enumerating some essential features of books of theology under any decent Christendom. Theology must present itself as the grandest form of knowledge. (It is the System on steroids.) It commands the most precise terminology, the most rigorous arguments, and the densest footnotes. Bibliographies—yes, obviously: immense listings in all the better human languages. Even the bindings on theological books ought to impress. The paper should feel expensive. The curated font must inspire confidence. In short, a tome that encourages you to put on white gloves before picking it up—or at least to sit up straight in your chair.

Unless our expectations for theology are exactly backward. Unless we need to be saved first of all from them—by returning to some honest philosophy.

Authors and Pseudonyms

Who would dare to write philosophical crumbs? The original title page names the author as Johannes Climacus, the publisher as S. Kierkegaard. Encouraged by their teachers, students of the book often overlook the complication. We know, "historically," that the work was written by Kierkegaard. Why he chose to attribute some of his works to other characters—well, we say, that's the "well-known problem" of Kierkegaard's pseudonyms. It has been magisterially resolved by attributing the views of the pseudonyms to various stages of the historical author's development. Or, perhaps, his excesses of compositional energy or a diagnosable graphomania. Poor Kierkegaard, always scribbling—because, you know, he was unlucky in love.

I ask, "Do we really want to begin our reading by dismissing the carefully constructed pseudonyms as entirely beside the main point? Do we just skip the title pages?"

"But," the magisterial interpretation continues (relinquishing just for a moment its favorite diagnoses), "Kierkegaard himself went on to write a book in which he assures us that the pseudonyms were a sort of aesthetic infatuation, a youthful extravagance, and then instructs us to read through the surface scenes for the familiar Christian message underneath."

I reply, "That's not what *Point of View for My Work as an Author* says. Even if it did, there is every reason to suppose that Kierkegaard could write ironically about his own writing. Instead of throwing out the pseudonyms to construct a unified system, arranged into biographical stages, we ought to assume that his compositional choices matter. If I am not the best reader, I want to remain for a little longer an apprentice reader. The title page of this little book says that it was written by Johannes Climacus."

Shaking its head, the magisterial interpretation abandons me as a hopeless case—and turns back to the more interesting problem of Kierkegaard's erotic frustrations.

I go back to the title page.

Who *is* Johannes Climacus? The expected answer would fill in the historical reference: Johannes Climacus, or John of the Ladder, was a monastic author in the Sinai during the sixth or seventh century who wrote a book that uses the image of Jacob's ladder to describe the soul's ascent to God. This "answer" only raises more questions. The author of *Philosophical Scraps* is evidently not a monk of old Sinai. He is a resident of modern Copenhagen. The original Johannes Climacus was an avowed Christian and sainted abbot; the author of this book is neither. Perhaps we are meant to understand the pseudonym from the first as a deliberate anachronism—a way of complicating the author's historical position. Or perhaps the pseudonym is not so much about the monastic author as about his famous book, the *Ladder*. The book we hold may be another ladder of ascent, offering to latter-day readers what the original book proposed to desert monks.

Turn the page and keep reading. The preface is—it should by now go without saying—curiously evasive. For example, it affronts the reader's expectations. The book is only "a little piece" that claims no place in scholarly striving (85). It is both too frivolous and too serious to be academic. On the one hand, it is casual, informal, occasional. Perhaps it is a "half-hour piece"—a *feuilleton* for the newspapers, a blog post. Quickly written to be read yet more quickly. It is play. It is a dance. On the other hand, in this dance Johannes stakes his life in ways that scholars rarely do, because he dances with the thought of death (87).

How to balance such contradictory characterizations? In the preface, a reader learns about three things: the present in which the piece appears; its author—Johannes himself; and the kind of reader that the piece wants. Together these points may prepare a reader to navigate the contradictory conditions for serious teaching.

The *present* is "a tumultuous age," a "circus-like time." It is animated by the "roaring insanity of a higher madness"; it exhibits "convulsive bellowing" and "irrational exaltation" (85–86). It loves portentous announcements and alarms—especially alarms. It races about in a flurry of activity and then declares the world-historical importance of its rushing. It eagerly awaits the system: the complete explanation of everything, especially its own preeminent position in history. Very serious business, the system. What a privilege to rush about in a city just about to receive it! Imagine the Fear Of Missing Out. It eats up all of your days and nights.

In the exhausting city, our *author* cuts a curious figure. A "comfortable idler" (85), Johannes Climacus is what his French contemporaries would call a *flâneur*, an urban stroller. He spends his time observing. Unmarried, not rich, he is unemployed or dubiously employed. He writes for his own amusement—and, curiously, for the honor of God. He serves at the altar in obedience to an unnamed master about whom he refuses to speak: "That is my business," he answers curtly (87).

This description resembles Plato's Socrates. Though married, Socrates lived his life as if single. He wandered the city, mocking it. When pressed, he claimed that he was responding to a divine command. Johannes Climacus may be what Socrates looks like in the Copenhagen of the 1830s. His book might then be a Platonic dialogue for that decade. Of course, many of the same descriptions apply to Jesus of Nazareth: unmarried, vagrant, often homeless, socially useless, occasionally mocking, obliged to perform a peculiar altar service without an altar in loving obedience to an occluded deity whom he calls Father. Johannes Climacus might be what Jesus looks like in Copenhagen's present; his book, a timely gospel.

The last thing in the preface is the *wished-for reader*, who will have both the freedom and the desire to unriddle a curious text. The wished-for reader is not the expected reader. The reader to be expected in modern Copenhagen will pick up the book just long enough to decide that it does not contain the long-expected System. He will then fling it aside before rushing on to a more promising new title. The wished-for reader appears less frequently and proceeds more slowly. Of course, even she may require a bit of reeducation before understanding *this* book.

Papier-Mâché Mask

The book is composed of scraps. They vary in genre. They interrupt one another. Just in the opening pages we find a guiding question, a motto from Shakespeare, a disjointed preface, and a *propositio*: each of the last three undoes the initial question. This composite opening is followed by five chapters. The first three are "a thought project," "a lyrical essay," and "a metaphysical caprice." The genre of the last two chapters is not specified, but both depict the relation of the disciple to a divine teacher who may already have appeared in history. Each chapter ends with a section in which an imagined reader objects to the book's progress. The exchanges between the author and this reader (expected and yet wished-for) go through stages. They mark the reader's reeducation.

There are further structural complications. Chapters 3, 4, and 5 are separated by sections labeled as additions or insertions. Between chapters 3 and 4, the interpolated section is an "addendum"; its subtitle is "An Acoustic Illusion." Between chapters 4 and 5, an interlude is likened to a musical piece that punctuates the acts of a comedy. After chapter 5, there is an enigmatic moral. Adding a moral draws attention to the text's possible effects on any reader who gets that far. What has the text done to the reader? And what is the reader supposed to do next?

None of the genre titles is specifically Christian. Neither is the playful arrangement, which breaks off into jokes. It is notorious that there is no record of Jesus laughing. Johannes does nothing but laugh—or smile, smirk, chuckle. His scene of instruction is a comic theater. Imitating Socrates, he underscores the affective contrast between Platonic scenes of instruction and their Christian successors. Or else he fashions a gaudy Platonic mask to hide the face of a Christian teacher.

Two Versions of Teaching

Philosophical Crumbs meditates on two interpretations of a scene of instruction. The scene is called the Moment. The interpretations are Hypothesis A and Hypothesis B. Johannes describes the difference between them repeatedly and variously. For example, it is the difference between the Socratic doctrine of recollection in the *Meno* (Hypothesis A) and something that sounds like a version of Christian incarnation (Hypothesis B). But the salient contrast between the two arises from how they value the Moment's pedagogical possibilities.

In Hypothesis A, the Moment "is *eo ipso* contingent, something vanishing, an occasion" (89). In Hypothesis B, by contrast, one moment is decisive because in it the divine Teacher meets a learner. The learner receives power to believe—and so enters into relation with the eternal through the Teacher. This one event is so important that "I could not for a moment forget it, neither in time nor in eternity, because the eternal, which did not exist before, came to be in this moment" (91).

This is theological language. Climacus introduces it hesitantly, hypothetically, because he means to de-familiarize it. Hypothesis B should appear only as the extremity of conceptual possibility. "But is that which has been developed here conceivable? We will not be hasty in answering" (97). Conceiving must stretch not just to salvation, or to the god appearing as a teacher, but to the character of the teaching moment itself. Is it conceivable that a pedagogical moment could be that decisive? If so, what happens to the sequence of our learning? Could the half hour (or lecture module) skeptically allotted to *Philosophical Crumbs* open onto an eternity? And what is teaching or Teaching in relation to eternity?

"Let us allow the god to go about the city in which he has appeared (which city it is does not matter)" (127). The god appears, teaches; the city reacts. The gossip about him (why not her?), the contradictory news, the consternation of religious authorities, the reaction of governmental powers far and near—none of this matters. The Teacher comes to meet an individual learner in a Moment that disrupts history as only eternity can. Compared to that disruption, everything else falls away.

Johannes's hypothesis about divine teaching underwrites a trenchant critique of modern biblical criticism. Imagine, he suggests, that you had the most complete historical record of the life of Jesus of Nazareth—to supply a name. Would that historical knowledge make you Jesus's disciple? No, of course not. On the contrary, discipleship needs even less of a historical record than is preserved in the canonical Gospels. You could lose Jesus's name, the places he lived ("which city it is does not matter"), major events of his life. What you need is only the claim that at some time, in some place, the eternal entered into history as a Teacher so that learners in history may find eternity. The scene of instruction fits within a single sentence.

Teaching in the Present

Let me now jump ahead, oh, eighteen hundred years. Or two thousand. It doesn't matter. The amount of intervening history also makes little difference. The fact that you live two millennia after the Teacher does not imply that you understand either less or more. The encouraging news is that you have not lost access to the original message. The bad news: you are not assured of being able to make better sense of it because you have new historical sciences or depth psychology. You are in almost exactly the same situation as you would have been two thousand years earlier. "Almost," because the further you are from the original shock of divine teaching, the more likely you are to be plunged into attempts to make it user-friendly. For example, there are these places called churches that offer cut-rate terms on relations with the eternal. Inside their gates, fluent chatter resounds: arguments of probability, assured methods for holiness, ranked pews, pins for perfect attendance, and certificates of orthodoxy. Or clubs for progressive solidarity, holistic wellness, and amateur theatricals (whether inside or outside worship). Some churches even deputize people to have your faith for you: they are called "clergy." Johannes can only shake his head. Better to feel the Moment's shock, to be knocked over by the tremor, to be offended at the paradox than to think that entering church gates will save you.

Any confidence that you could fellowship your way to God is dangerous. Wrestle, instead and in silence, with a single sentence passed down from an otherwise erased past: "We believe that the god, *anno* this or that, appeared in the lowly form of a servant, lived and taught among us, and then died" (167). The only thing that one generation can say to another, that one person can say to another, is, "I believe and have believed, that this has happened, *despite the fact that it is foolishness to the understanding and an offence to the human heart*" (165–66).

Writing in the Present

Johannes Climacus doesn't write those words except indirectly, in quotation marks. But he does write many others in his own voice. How can he justify his writing if he is so worried that chatter will distract from the Moment?

Perhaps he has not yet reached the Moment. Or perhaps our condition as readers is such that we could not understand truer words if he wrote them plainly, in all earnestness, without some preparation. We are so filled with chatter that he must smile, smirk, chuckle in order to entertain us while he tries to figure out how to pierce our comfortably uncomfortable distraction. Or perhaps we would judge that we had already heard those (Christian) words—those tedious clichés drilled into some of us during childhood or broadcast endlessly to adults by well-dressed "evangelists." End of half hour! On to the next sighting of a System that could save us!

Or perhaps there is no saving the familiar Christian words now. Perhaps we can only use them in quotation marks, as a thought experiment. The chatter may have so corrupted them that they can only be overheard, glimpsed from the corner of the eye like a highway billboard flashing by at night. Perhaps the old structures must be leveled, the canonical words suspended, before God works in some new way to grant the condition of learning in the Moment. Imagine a last generation so late in time, so engulfed by chatter, that it can hear a profession of faith only when it appears as an ironic question posed by a writer who will never claim to be a Christian.

16

Simone Weil,
Letters and Essays

In the last century, a girl was born into a religiously nonobservant family.[1] She grew up without toys or dolls—by her mother's design. She was precocious in her dedication to intellectual life, including poetry and other literature, though she always felt herself overshadowed by her brother, a mathematical prodigy. At the age of fourteen, she considered killing herself because of the "mediocrity" of her "natural faculties" (768–69). Instead, she went on to victory in various academic races. She graduated from one of her country's most prestigious academic institutions, where she wrote a thesis on beauty.

She devoted herself increasingly to political struggles on behalf of the industrialized poor. The struggles gave scope to her gift for dramatic stubbornness. During a labor dispute at her famous school, for example, she organized a collection on behalf of striking staff. The head of the school gave her a small contribution on condition that it be kept anonymous. The young woman (no longer a girl) immediately put up posters that read: "Follow the example of your director. Give anonymously to the strike fund!" (46).

After graduation, she was assigned to a series of secondary schools. She taught philosophy, Greek, and history, but offered extracurricular electives on the history of science. In her spare time, she tutored laborers for free. Her political activities got her into trouble with educational bureaucrats, though often not with her students or (surprisingly) their parents. She finally left teaching because of failing health. She continued to write for militant newspapers and political journals.

When her country was invaded by fascist racists, following a collapse of the international order that she had predicted, she was forced to flee. Once again, she insisted on physical identification with those in distress: she refused to eat more than the rations allotted her compatriots in the occupied homeland. She died of heart failure at the age of thirty-four. The coroner's report read in part, "the deceased did kill and slay herself by refusing to eat whilst the balance of her mind was disturbed."[2] She was, in the coroner's sober judgment, a madwoman. It is worth reflecting on that psychiatric diagnosis of a life given over to learning and teaching.

I am telling some of the life of Simone Weil—telling it in ways she might once have approved, though she would by the end of her life have objected to important omissions. Weil has many claims to be a modern political writer—and perhaps a political martyr. That is not why she is read so avidly today. She is now famous as a Christian author—indeed, a Catholic one. The identification is and is not true.

Slowly, this teacher of philosophy was taught by God. (In the language of Johannes Climacus, her Moment stretched across years of historical time.) The instruction remained private. Though she pestered numerous Catholic priests with questions and spent more time at liturgies than many of the devout, she refused baptism. She never passed through church gates except as a visitor. The refusal did not express loyalty to her Jewish origin. On the contrary, Weil was intolerant toward both modern Judaism and the Hebrew Bible. Though she was a target for many varieties of anti-Semitism, from petty name-calling to genocide, she remained willfully blind to it. Nor was Weil's refusal of baptism an ordinary distaste for the failings of Christian churches—however unsparing she was when describing them. Weil refused to be baptized because she thought that Christian churches excluded too many divine beauties.

In her writings, Weil contrasts the limited view of any Christian church with the universality of God's creation and call. "Christianity is catholic [that is, universal] by right but not in fact. So many things are outside it, so many things that I love and do not want to give up, so many things that God loves, otherwise they would be without existence" (775). Again, "the beauty of the world, the pure and authentic reflections of this beauty in the arts and in science, the spectacle of the folds of the human heart in hearts empty of religious belief, all these things have done as much as visibly Christian ones to deliver me a captive to Christ. I think I might even say [that they did] more" (785). If Weil's life contains a conversion story, it ends with a resolution to remain outside any official church body—precisely as a witness to the wholeness of divine pedagogy.

A Conversion Narrative?

Simone Weil wrote an autobiographical letter as she prepared to flee Marseille for New York with her parents. Mistrusting the Vichy "Free Zone," the three of them had always planned to leave it for the United States once they secured visas. While in Marseille, Simone Weil met Joseph-Marie Perrin, a Dominican priest committed to lay spirituality. She addressed her letter to him. Though he published it under the title "Spiritual Autobiography," Weil announces a different purpose within the text. She acknowledges her spiritual debt to Perrin even while she justifies her refusal to be baptized by him. She narrates three decisive contacts with Catholicism: at a saint's festival in a Portuguese village, during two days in Assisi, and over Holy Week at the abbey of Solesmes. They are three scenes of instruction through divine beauty.

Portugal: Weil's solicitous parents have taken her away to rest after her labor in a Renault factory. One night on the Atlantic coast, under a full moon, she listens as women sing with heart-tearing sadness, going in procession from boat to boat. This can sound like a sentimental tourist vignette. Weil's reaction is different. In that moment, she is moved by beauty to know that

"Christianity is pre-eminently the religion of slaves, that slaves cannot help but belong to it, and I among others" (771). Weil paraphrases Nietzsche to rebuke him.

Two years later, Weil spends a few days in Assisi. At one point, she enters the Porziuncola, a rough Romanesque chapel now encased by a neoclassical basilica of improbable pastels. The small chapel has been preserved because Saint Francis rebuilt it with his own hands. In that chapel, Weil is "compelled . . . for the first time in [her] life to go down on [her] knees" in prayer (771). Compelled by what? By something "stronger than [she] was."

One year after the visit to Assisi, Weil spends Holy Week at the Benedictine abbey of Solesmes, famous for its restoration of monastic liturgy. It becomes for her a third scene of instruction. The purified performance of ancient song in an austere church was indeed beautiful to her, but not only in the ways we diminish by calling "aesthetic." She hears, from a young English visitor, of the poet George Herbert. She memorizes and begins regularly to recite one of Herbert's poems. Suddenly, during a recitation at an unspecified time, in an unspecified place, "Christ himself came down and took possession of [her]." She had never foreseen the possibility "of a real contact, person to person." "In this sudden possession of me by Christ, neither my senses nor my imagination had any part; I only felt through my suffering the presence of love, analogous to that which one can read in the smile of a beloved face" (771–72). Without senses or imagination, she feels love in suffering—then "reads" it as a loving smile, as wordless expression.

Beauties deliver Weil "to Christ" because she realizes that "sensible and contingent beauty [is] perceived through the net of chance and evil" (to borrow words from another of her texts).[3] Beauty can be found even in representations of horrifying reality. Her regular example is Homer's *Iliad*. The example points to what is most disconcerting in Weil's conception of divine beauty. Under the circumstances of our history—especially in an age of industrialized tyrannies—divine love may appear most vividly *only* in the middle of suffering.

A Mystical Narrative?

In the letter to Perrin, Weil refers several times to the decisive role of affliction (*malheur*) in her life. Contact with affliction in the factory "killed her youth." She became part of the anonymous mass: "the affliction of others entered into my flesh and my soul. Nothing separated me from it, for I had really forgotten my past and I awaited no future" (770). "Entered into my flesh and my soul"—this is very like the language she uses to describe her association with Christ's passion during Holy Week. The affliction of the factory somehow resembles the arrival of Christ.

Elsewhere Weil tries to represent affliction more precisely—to serve beauty even when rendering affliction. Affliction stands out from other suffering in the totality of its assault on the human being: physical pain, distress of soul, social degradation all at once. It provokes scorn, revulsion, hatred—against the afflicted, but also within them, whenever they look on themselves or the world. It leaves permanent effects: its scars cannot be removed during the present life even by God. Most of all, affliction exceeds other suffering in its mechanical operation: it smashes human lives randomly, like the stamping of rogue machines.

Where is beauty in this? It would be obscene to declare that affliction simply *is* beautiful. If it were, Weil could pull up a chair to watch the degradation of workers in factories as performance art. She claims instead that divine beauty survives whatever defacements human history inflicts on it. Christ's execution is intended to be fearsomely ugly—and yet a greater beauty springs forth. Of course, that claim runs an enormous pedagogical risk in hopes of a greater learning. The risk is that the afflicted will stop loving altogether, and so make God's perceived absence final. The possibility, tangled inextricably with the risk, is that individual affliction might be joined to the great cosmic suffering—the separation of God from God in the drama of redemption—and so be carried into God's inner life.[4]

The pedagogical risk is quite real for Weil. She believes that one gesture—a discipline, an art—might increase the chance of turning it toward salvation. She calls it attention. Weil places the highest value on it. A quarter hour of deliberate attention counts, she insists, as much as many good works. She also links attention to love. The most hopeful response to affliction is to continue loving right through it: "The soul must continue to love in the emptiness, or at least to will to love, even if only with an infinitesimal part of herself. Then one day God will come to show himself to her and to reveal the beauty of the world, as happened with Job" (695). Beauty is not only a means of finding God. It is God's response to the cry of the afflicted.

For Weil, attention during affliction becomes an imperative to write. Write she did, for political campaigns and academic reviews, but even more in letters, journals, essays never particularly intended for publication. Why write—or teach? Not to systematize affliction, which cannot be articulated either by those undergoing it or by those standing alongside.[5] Weil's writing may instead help her—or her best reader—in paying steadier attention to the afflicted (including, sometimes, oneself). Paying attention to someone under affliction is, properly speaking, a miracle. Weil wants to elicit the miracle by writing and teaching.

At the core of the Catholic practice that she will not join is something stripped of evident beauty. This is the eucharistic "host" or wafer: a little stuff, a bit of bread, a crumb. Even for those who receive communion, the task is still to wait in darkness: "It is for them to remain motionless, without averting their eyes, listening ceaselessly, and waiting, they know not for what; deaf to entreaties and threats, unmoved by every shock, unshaken in the midst of every upheaval" (761). Weil redoubles their tense expectation—because she is not even at the communion rail. She sits at the back of the church, having slipped through the gates for a visit. She still waits to assume her place among those who attend to "they know not what" in repeating Jesus's table ritual.

If I admire Weil's aching descriptions of contacts with beauty, I admire even more her refusal to *stop* waiting on them.

17

Locked Gates

In his final book about Narnia, *The Last Battle*, C. S. Lewis tells of a stable with an "inside bigger than its outside." Lucy, now fully a queen, agrees: "In our world too, a Stable once had something inside it that was bigger than our whole world."[1] She means the stable in Bethlehem, of course. But the figure, as Lewis intends, has wide application. Churches are supposed to be larger than their buildings—though many congregations are now dwarfed by the edifices they struggle to maintain. Seminaries, too, should be larger inside than out, since Christian scenes of instruction expand unpredictably for those who enter them.

I share Weil's sadness that Christian institutions are often smaller than what they profess. She complained of all the beauties excluded by the asserted "catholicity" of some Christian churches. I would repeat, in my idiom, that church gates shut out so many scenes of divine instruction. The policing that wants to keep dangerous heresies or scandals safely outside constricts the "orthodoxy" taught within. Scenes of Christian instruction do not work well under aggressive surveillance.

Policing Tradition

Much church talk about ministerial formation traffics in fantasies. It wishes for a theological tradition that can be owned with confidence before being transferred to a new owner—accompanied by a limited warranty and litigation-proof directions for proper use.

I can illustrate the twofold fantasy from a terrible course I once offered. As an inexperienced and newly arrived faculty member, I was assigned to teach "The Scholastic Tradition" to a group of Roman Catholic seminarians. No further explanation of the course was offered, and I stupidly didn't ask for any. I set about designing a one-semester survey that would move from Thomas Aquinas through seven centuries of commentary and controversy up to the Second Vatican Council. No small task. I threw together the lectures from week to week by scavenging whatever I could find.

Around the middle of the semester—I recall that the class had reached the more technical differences between Bañez and Molina on grace—my chairman called me in to tell me what I already felt: the course was indeed a failure. He explained that "Scholastic Tradition" was not supposed to be a historical survey, but a drill in basic terms and concepts. The course had typically been taught from mimeographed sheets of definitions that the students were asked to memorize. "All we want," my chairman concluded, "is for the seminarians to learn the basics of Scholasticism."

Embarrassed but not yet flattened, I blurted out, "But *whose* Scholasticism? Which one?"

In this exchange, you can see one fantasy of tradition as definite content and another of its predictable transfer. My long-suffering chairman, no doubt receiving daily calls of complaint, just wanted the seminarians to acquire a few dozen technical terms and some quick outlines of standard arguments. Still, he really did believe that there was a recognizable content called "the Scholastic tradition." I did not believe that. I still don't. The Scholastic tradition is a crowd of disputes in which the most vigorously controverted question remains: Who counts as a true Scholastic?

Unfortunately, my clumsy course-design missed the pedagogical implications of my own view. I had failed to imagine a way to introduce the best-disposed students into a living "tradition," much less to persuade ill-disposed students to take any interest in it. If a tradition is an anthology of open scenes of instruction, it cannot be taught as a chronology of settled positions. A living tradition can never be surveyed; it can only be inhabited. A dead tradition is no longer a tradition.

The claim may sound like a flimsy platitude, but it still proves controversial when applied to ministerial education. Often when church people speak of the tradition—especially when their tone of voice or a roll of the eyes implies capital letters, The Tradition—the last thing they mean is the *activity* of Christian thinking over centuries. They picture instead freeze-dried doctrine, an official story packaged by decree. It is prudent for ministerial candidates to learn a handful of doctrines and stories. They will encounter them again during the ordination process and in congregational life. Still, I want to distinguish current promulgations of The Tradition from living engagements with the luminous and startling lives found in Christian scenes of instruction.

Heresy, Mystery, Eschatology

But, you may object, aren't there errors of Christian thinking against which the teaching of theology must guard?

There are, I believe, ways of teaching theology that are dangerous. Since no human formulae (including the Scriptures) can be wholly adequate to divinity, I do not consider these "errors" in any ordinary sense. An error in theology is not like adding up a column of figures incorrectly or mistaking the current postmaster general. It is more like going far out of your way to reach an urgent destination. Or it is like using needlessly complicated sentences to give important advice. Or it is like doing something hurtful to your lover in the name of a "principle" that is actually your vanity. Straining to secure propositional orthodoxy, we regularly succumb to pedagogical heresy. How we teach theology too often undoes the good that might come from what we teach.

Theology is ongoing instruction for getting you to a way of life that you deeply desire but often misapprehend and sometimes flee in self-hatred. When "theology" becomes something else, it becomes less useful—or even useless—for reaching its end. The antidote typically has more to do with dispositions, motives, and virtues or vices than with propositional entailments. How could it be otherwise for teaching that is a divine gift? Some people perform verbal orthodoxy in cynicism or despair—because it is easier to memorize the catechism or code of canon law than to wait on God.

If Johannes Climacus and Weil disagree on many things, they agree emphatically on the importance of waiting without chatter for the eternal to touch time, whether as Teacher or in a little piece of bread. That moment is a future for which human teachers can only prepare.

Exercise: Pay attention for fifteen minutes to one scene of instruction that you are trying to teach—and only to it.

Exercise: Take a leisurely stroll in your neighborhood, without earbuds or headphones, scouting for signs of the Teacher. Pay no attention to alarms, advertisements, or television screens. Come back to your writing place. Listen for the voice that comes out—even if it seems to be not exactly yours. Whose might it be? Should you give the speaker a name?

Conclusion

Finding or Making Shelter

Unless you jumped directly to this conclusion, you have been reading pages that reactivate powerful scenes of Christian instruction—some old, some recent. I won't summarize them—indeed, I can't. Either the scenes have exerted their attractions or they haven't. If they have, a summary would be silly. If they haven't, it would be pointless.

Having tried to move us both into these scenes, I have emphasized their differences while showing my embracing reactions. Most of the authors I have recalled are my models. I have other models, of course, so many that they would overfill a much thicker book. Still, most of the texts I have tried to vivify in this short book have been my own scenes of instruction during many years. Choosing them, I am sure to have disagreed with your choices. I have almost certainly left out some of your favorite scenes. Worse, I may have included a writer whom you regard as a very bad teacher. I do apologize. Then I remind you that this book has accomplished something even if it leads you to reactivate your favorite scenes just to show how good they are.

Attending to teaching, we reverse the perspective in many anxious quarrels about the decline of theological education. It may seem too embarrassingly obvious to remark that any future for theological education must be a future of teaching. But the remark is no longer obvious, if it ever was. It figures too rarely in our debates about theological education. When it does appear, it is often treated as self-explanatory. As if there were no serious questions about how it becomes possible to teach theology. As if such teaching were a rudimentary skill that could be relayed to anyone in easy lessons. However we resolve the institutional future of theological education, we cannot go forward into it without asking hard questions about teaching.

Let me say this again, with an example. If you ask, "*Where* is Christian teaching done?," the least misleading answer is, "In scenes of instruction." It can sometimes also be true to say, "It is done in those buildings over there," or, "It happens at that institution." Still, those responses take two or three giant steps back from the center of theology. I wouldn't scruple over this distinction except that forgetting it has consequences. Very often, talk about schools of theology proceeds on the assumption that they must be like other professional schools. Each one will need a governance structure, a teaching staff, adequate buildings, a sizable library, an admissions office, HR managers, outcome measures and risk assessments . . . But Christian scenes of instruction *require* none of those things.

Christian teaching has come to life in very different sorts of institutions, because an institution, as much as a building, is a different sort of thing from a theological scene. Scenes are composed and usually conducted by human beings, who must wait on the divine for completion. The physical and institutional emplacement of the scene is both secondary and historically variable. Secondary and variable, but not negligible. Each of the scenes we have watched required time for enacting or writing, then more time for reading, meditating, discussing. Time for teaching or learning is expensive. Someone must pay for it and then protect it if teaching is to be more than episodic. There are other needs as well—and many other practical skills—in running anything like a school. Still, the shape of the school, including its economic arrangements, cannot be *deduced* from the scenes taught within it. A scene of instruction does not dictate plans for governance or fund-raising. It will not even yield a detailed curriculum with fixed outcomes. Any number of institutional forms have served admirably over centuries to shelter theological scenes. (Are we really convinced that we teach Christian theology better now than others did in earlier times and other places?) The decisive thing for theological education is not a specific institutional structure, business model, or curriculum.

On the other hand, institutional structures or habits can make it *harder* to reactivate scenes of instruction. I have described some of the difficulties on earlier pages, and I could bring them together in a bit of advice. A school that wants to house theological scenes must encourage bodily habituation by ethical training and ritual. It must authorize theology to have flexible relations with adjacent arts and sciences, so that it can engage them without being subordinated to them. If an institution wants to accommodate the teaching of Christian theology, it must encourage robust exercises of imagination and the kinds of writing that go with them. It must welcome strong pedagogies that cultivate resistance and avoid abuse. What is most important, the school must not try to circumscribe the effects of what it teaches. It must not lock the gates against the future.

These remarks are vague because they are general. I am happy to leave them that way, because I believe we now need the widest range of experiments with institutional form. As an insatiable reader of old books, I do wonder whether we might usefully return to some relinquished models for teaching theology: apprenticeships, intentional communities, houses of study alongside universities. But that is only today's list of my favorites. We need as many experiments with structures for sheltering theology as we can manage—with or without the blessing of accreditation and (forgive me) denominational approval. We also need experiments in writing. The page remains a powerful space for pedagogical experiments. (An argument for more attentive theological teaching by scenes is also an argument for different genres of writing.) If the future of theological education in the United States looks to be poorer and smaller than what it has been, we might relearn from poor and small communities the power of the Word.

The changes in theological institutions that now frighten us are mostly irreversible. We may need to lament real losses for a while, but we should also see that some institutional "losses" are gains for teaching. In their desperation to survive within the larger economies of technocratic education, some institutions have moved to the least hopeful versions of the professional model for ministerial education.[1] If I cannot see the future, I hope to be able to read parts of the present. In our present, right before our eyes, some institutional choices for institutional survival at any cost have made it very difficult to teach theology.

I do not think that is what Schleiermacher meant, but that is what Schleiermacher's compromise with professional education has sometimes become, inside and outside universities. It is our technocratic versions that I have in mind when I say that the future of theological education actually needs to be the opposite of professional. We need to focus not on the standards of professional training issued this week by the ranked schools, placement agencies, or national accrediting bodies. We need instead to experiment with institutions—of many kinds—that encourage the most serious teaching of theology, in the confidence that theological teaching is not merely a human enterprise. I go further. What Christian theology can contribute to universities or intellectual life more broadly is a practice of resistance to conceptions of education as the efficient transmission of testable information. Strong faculties of theology in universities—or strong free-standing seminaries—must resist the trivialization of teaching. The schools stay strong not by chasing after the latest models of training but by paying steady attention to the living scenes in which teaching happens when learners are changed—and not chiefly by human management. We like to say, quoting Anselm, who is paraphrasing Augustine, that theology is "faith seeking understanding." Theology can seek only because believers have already been sought—by God, who took our flesh.

For Further Thought

The reader will find here suggestions for further reading. The suggestions are meant seriously. This book, more than most I have written, is not a sealed space, complete in itself. It means to pose questions for a future that it cannot yet see.

Throughout this short book, I have argued that books *about* teaching are often less helpful than books *that teach*. Many of the canonical works of Christian theology provide patterns for our teaching in the ways that they teach us. So, when we look for help with our teaching, we could do much worse than begin with the books that we are trying to teach. I've tried to show this in some of the texts that I teach eagerly, but the suggestion will be more convincing if you apply it to books that you love to teach. Reread the book not for its "content"—much less for its historical "context"—but as a tutorial in how to teach.

Many years ago, a colleague in my school's teaching training program used to teach a course on the philosophy of education with just three texts: Plato's *Republic*, Rousseau's *Émile*, and Dewey's *Democracy and Education*. Another exercise you might perform is to imagine a course on the theology of theological education with just three titles, drawn from widely spaced centuries.

Of course, sometimes we need books that help us reflect most particularly on teaching in our daily circumstances—in the schools that we now inhabit. Since I conceive theological education as inevitably resistant to most of the reigning educational models, I often find help in generous critiques of standard teaching. Here are five of the books I've read and reread while trying to write on theological education.

Brann, Eva T. H. *Paradoxes of Education in a Republic*. Chicago: University of Chicago Press, 2002.

Freire, Paolo. *Pedagogy of the Oppressed*. Translated by Myra Bergman Ramos. New York: Seabury, 1970.

Goodman, Paul. *Compulsory Mis-education*. New York: Horizon, 1964.

hooks, bell. *Teaching to Transgress: Education as the Practice of Freedom*. New York: Routledge, 1994.

Illich, Ivan. *Deschooling Society*. New York: Harper & Row, 1971.

As often happens in reading, I learn best from some of these authors where we disagree most. So, here too I urge you to erase my list and make your own.

Your collaboration with this book will carry forward the process of its composition. More than any other I've written, the book has benefited from patient conversation. I owe a special debt to comments by the earliest test-readers, fellow members of a group that gathered over several years under the phrase that has become our series title, Theological Education between the Times. We understood it at once as a question and an affirmation.

Notes

Chapter 1

1. Soko Morinaga reports some Zen advice: "disciples fall into three categories, based upon their relations with their teacher: The best students are attached by hatred, the mediocre by charity, and the worst by authority" (*Novice to Master: An Ongoing Lesson in the Extent of My Own Stupidity* [Somerville, MA: Wisdom Publications, 2004], 57). I am too thin-skinned to stir up hatred deliberately, but I try hard to remember the range a student's emotions must pass through in our meetings.

2. This is the account of Samuel H. Scudder (writing as A Former Pupil), "In the Laboratory with Agassiz," *American Poems*, 23rd ed. (Boston: Houghton, Osgood & Co., 1879), 450–54. For another version, see Ezra Pound, *ABC of Reading* (New Haven: Yale University Press, 1934), 3–4. In 1896, William James remarked, "There is probably no public school teacher now in New England who will not tell you how Agassiz used to lock a student up in a room full of turtle shells, or lobster shells, or oyster shells, without a book or word to help him, and not let him out till he had discovered all the truths which the objects contained." *Louis Agassiz: words spoken by Professor William James at the reception of the American Society of Naturalists by the president and fellows of Harvard University at Cambridge, on December 30, 1896* (Cambridge, MA: Harvard University, 1897), 9.

3. I translate from Friedrich Schleiermacher, *Kurze Darstellung des theologischen Studiums* (1811), ed. Dirk Schmid, in *Kritische Gesamtausgabe* (Berlin: de Gruyter, 1980–), I/6: *Schriften und Entwürfe*, introduction ##1, 5–6, pp. 249–50. In this section, I refer to the pages of this work parenthetically.

4. Schleiermacher makes the exclusion of liturgy and other "symbolic

actions" explicit in the 1830 version of this part of the text (*Kritische Gesamt-ausgabe* I/6, 326).

Chapter 2

1. Throughout the book, translations of the New Testament are my own. So, obviously, are any typographical emphases in them.

2. For more on ancient philosophical scenes, see the discussion in my *Teaching Bodies: Moral Formation in the Summa of Thomas Aquinas* (New York: Fordham University Press, 2017), 68–79.

3. My colleague Charles Hallisey compares this to one of the features of the world imagined by George Saunders, *Lincoln in the Bardo* (New York: Random House, 2017). When the dead engage Abraham Lincoln during his visits to the cemetery, they also learn what has been going on among the living since their departure.

4. Dietrich Bonhoeffer, *Discipleship* (Minneapolis: Fortress, 2003), 87, with note 1.

5. Ben Lerner, *The Hatred of Poetry* (London: Fitzcarraldo Editions, 2017), 10, 14, and 18, respectively.

Chapter 3

1. The work has been titled *Life of Macrina*. I translate from the Greek in *Vita S. Macrinae*, ed. Virginia Woods Callahan, *Gregorii Nysseni opera* 8/1 (Leiden: Brill, 1952). In this chapter, I refer to the work's standard sections parenthetically. For a lively English translation, see the rendering by Kevin Corrigan (Toronto: Peregrina, 1997).

Chapter 4

1. In this chapter, I refer parenthetically to the page numbers of Althaus-Reid, *Indecent Theology: Theological Perversions in Sex, Gender, and Politics* (London: Routledge, 2000). When several phrases are quoted in series from the same page, I cite the number only for the first of them. I acknowledge a special debt to Hannah Hofheinz, who taught me to reread *Indecent Theology*. Those lessons and much more are contained in "Implicate and Trans-

gress: Marcella Althaus-Reid, Writing, and a Transformation of Theological Knowledge" (PhD diss., Harvard University, 2015).

2. Althaus-Reid quotes from the song "D.L.G.," released on the album *Giros* in 1985. "D.L.G." abbreviates *Dia de los Grones*. *Grones* is an anagram for *Negros*, which means (literally) persons of African descent but (analogically) any "animal of work" (as the song says). Althaus-Reid paraphrases: "the humble ones, the poor, the oppressed" (121).

Chapter 6

1. I follow *Legenda major* 13.2–3, as in Bonaventure, *Opera omnia*, ed. Patres Collegii Sancti Bonaventurae, vol. 8 (Quaracchi, Italy: CSB, 1898), 504–64. There is an English version in the Paulist Press volume cited in the next note.

2. I cite quotations by traditional chapter and section numbers of the *Itinerarium mentis in Deum*, translating from the text in Bonaventure, *Opera omnia*, ed. Patres Collegii Sancti Bonaventurae, vol. 5 (Quaracchi, Italy: CSB, 1891), 293–316. I usually teach the *Itinerarium* from *Bonaventure: The Soul's Journey into God, The Tree of Life, The Life of St. Francis*, ed. and trans. Ewert Cousins (New York: Paulist, 1978). With every translation in this chapter, I suffer the clumsy inadequacy of my English renderings of Bonaventure's compact and luminous poetry.

Chapter 7

1. Paul Tillich, *The Courage to Be*, 3rd ed. (New Haven: Yale University Press, 2014). In this chapter, I give page references from this work parenthetically.

2. Harvey Cox, "Introduction to the Third Edition," in Tillich, *The Courage to Be*, xi–xii. I play off of Cox's opening in my own. Elsewhere, Cox raises astute questions about the rhetorical effectiveness of *Courage*. See Cox, *The Secular City: Secularization and Urbanization in Theological Perspective* (Princeton: Princeton University Press, 2013), 93–97.

3. For the purpose of the Terry Lectures, see the deed of gift as quoted on the lectureship's website, http://terrylecture.yale.edu/about-dwight-h-terry -lectureship.

4. *Time* 73, no. 11 (March 16, 1959).

5. For the quotations on the arts, see Paul Tillich, *On the Boundary: An Autobiographical Sketch* (New York: Scribner's Sons, 1966), 28, 52. For synthesis and system in these limit cases, see his *My Search for Absolutes* (New York: Simon & Schuster, 1967), 46.

Chapter 8

1. I rewrite Adam Phillips, *On Kissing, Tickling, and Being Bored: Psychoanalytic Essays on the Unexamined Life* (Cambridge MA: Harvard University Press, 1993), 4.

Chapter 9

1. Augusto Boal, *Theatre of the Oppressed* (New York: Theatre Communications Group, 1985), especially 126–55.

2. Teresa of Ávila, *Moradas de castillo interior*, as in *Santa Teresa de Jesús: Obras completas*, ed. Efrén de la Madre de Dios and Otger Steggink (Madrid: Biblioteca de Autores Cristianos, 2015), prologue no. 5, p. 471. I usually teach this text in the translation by Kieran Kavanaugh and Otilio Rodriguez (Mahwah, NJ: Paulist, 1979).

Chapter 10

1. In this chapter, I refer parenthetically to pages in John Bunyan, *The Pilgrim's Progress: From This World to That Which Is to Come*, ed. James Blanton Wharey, rev. Roger Sharrock, 2nd rev. ed. (Oxford: Clarendon, 1967).

2. Anthony Powell, *A Dance to the Music of Time*, vol. 12, *Hearing Secret Harmonies* (Chicago: University of Chicago Press, 1995), chap. 6, pp. 233–34.

3. The bibliographical evidence is a bit more confusing than my quick summary suggests. See the introductory notes, pp. xxxix, l, liii, and so on.

Chapter 11

1. Susan Sontag, *Under the Sign of Saturn* (New York: Farrar, Straus & Giroux, 1980), 129.

2. The notion of "literary montage" is developed in Benjamin, "Das Passagenwerk," in *Gesammelte Schriften*, ed. Rolf Teidemann, vol. 5/1 (Frankfurt: Suhrkamp, 1982), 572–74, especially frags. N1, 10, and N1A, 8. The quotation on "Waking" appears on 556–57, frag. N2a, 3. I follow the text of the theses in *Gesammelte Schriften*, 1:691–704.

Chapter 12

1. Among the many editions, I refer to C. S. Lewis, *The Lion, the Witch and the Wardrobe*, illustrated by Pauline Baynes (London: Geoffrey Bles, 1950). In this chapter, I refer to the pages of the edition parenthetically.

2. See Lewis's introduction to George MacDonald, *Phantastes: A Faerie Romance* (Grand Rapids: Eerdmans, 2000), x.

3. I quote the two phrases from the Chicago-Lambeth Quadrilateral, in the version adopted by the Lambeth Conference of 1888 (in Resolution 11).

Chapter 13

1. Octavia Butler, *Parable of the Sower* (New York: Warner Books, 2000). In this chapter, I give page references from this text parenthetically.

2. Samuel Delany and Robert Reid-Pharr, "Sex, Race, and Science Fiction: The Callaloo Interview," in Delany, *Silent Interviews* (Hanover, NH: Wesleyan University Press / University Press of New England, 1994), 216–29, at 224–25.

3. Joan Fry, "'Congratulations! You've Just Won $295,000!': An Interview with Octavia E. Butler," *Poets and Writers* 25, no. 2 (March/April 1997): 58–69, reprinted in *Conversations with Octavia Butler* (Jackson: University of Mississippi Press, 2010), 123–33.

4. In the online exhibit at http://www.huntington.org/octaviabutler/ (accessed March 27, 2020).

Chapter 14

1. Michel Foucault, *Sécurité, territoire, population: Cours au Collège de France, 1977–78*, ed. Michel Senellart, dir. François Ewald and Alessandro Fontana (Paris: Gallimard and Seuil, 2004), 198–99, 204–5.

Chapter 15

1. Søren Kierkegaard, *Philosophical Crumbs*, in his *Repetition and Philosophical Crumbs*, trans. M. G. Piety (Oxford: Oxford University Press, 2009), 85. In this chapter, I give page references from this work parenthetically. Unable to read Danish, I choose the translation recommended to me by a former student who does and who has written convincingly about Kierkegaard's authorship: Carl Hughes, *Kierkegaard and the Staging of Desire: Rhetoric and Performance in a Theology of Eros* (New York: Fordham University Press, 2014).

Chapter 16

1. The girl is Simone Weil. In this chapter, I will cite her work parenthetically from *Œuvres*, ed. Florence de Lussy (Paris: Quarto / Gallimard, 1999). I also rely on this book's illustrated chronology (37–93).
2. Francine du Plessix Gray, *Simone Weil* (New York: Viking Penguin, 2001), 212.
3. Simone Weil, *La Pesanteur et la grâce* (Paris: Plon, 1948), 170.
4. For the points in this paragraph, see Weil, "L'amour de Dieu," in *Œuvres*, 695, 698–99, 703–4.
5. Simone Weil, "La personne et le sacré: Collectivité—personne—impersonnel—droit-justice," in her *Écrits de Londres et dernières lettres* (Paris: Gallimard, 1957), 11–44, at 14 and 28–29.

Chapter 17

1. C. S. Lewis, *The Last Battle* (London: Bodley Head, 1956), 133.

Conclusion

1. Here I allude with gratitude to Ted Smith's critical history (in the most robust sense) of the rise and fall of the professional model of Christian ministry. He presents one version of the argument in his book for this series.